INTRODUCING THE MEDIEVAL DRAGON

INTRODUCING THE MEDIEVAL DRAGON

THOMAS HONEGGER

UNIVERSITY OF WALES PRESS

www.uwp.co.uk
British Library CIP *Data*

A catalogue record for this book is available from the British Library
ISBN 978-1-78683-468-3
eISBN 978-1-78683-469-0

Designed and typeset by Chris Bell, cbdesign
Printed by the CPI Antony Rowe, Melksham

To Saint Margaret of Antioch
(alias Saint Marina the Great Martyr) –
and to her namesakes

SERIES EDITORS' PREFACE

THE UNIVERSITY OF WALES Press series on Medieval Animals explores the historical and cultural impact of animals in this formative period, with the aim of developing new insights, analysing cultural, social and theological tensions and revealing their remarkable resonances with our contemporary world. The series investigates ideas about animals in medieval Europe, from the fifth century to the sixteenth. Medieval thought on animals benefitted from a rich classical inheritance, and some attitudes towards animals that we might consider as having characterized the Middle Ages persisted up to the Enlightenment era – and even to the present day.

When we think about medieval animals, we might variously mean livestock, individual specimens of the genus or species in a particular historical era, or the companion and support to practical human concerns ranging from travel to arable harvests; we might also speak of symbolic creatures and emblems, fictional creatures whose existence is rooted in medieval imagination, the bestiary creature lauded or disparaged for its association with culturally coded behavioural traits, or the animal of natural hierarchy who provides the philosophical and symbolic counterpoint to reason or civilization – the animal as nonhuman. The titles in the series therefore engage with theoretical perspectives and philosophical questions from both the medieval and modern eras, with a concern for intersectional approaches bringing together animality with studies of gender, sexuality, race and postcolonial theory. They build on the diverse and influential reflexes of the 'animal turn' in critical theory and humanities scholarship, encompassing both *animality studies* (on the relation of human and animal in cultural studies) and *animal studies* (with its concomitant considerations for non-human advocacy).

A range of different formats has been chosen to reflect the diversity of the medieval primary sources and the wide interdisciplinary academic research they have inspired which will encourage a general readership through pithy, accessible and appealing books. Medieval Animals is the first series to systematically explore the roles and perceptions of individual animals during the Middle Ages. The 'Introducing…' titles focus on the importance of specific animals in art, literature and history; the primary sources reader is designed to support deeper and broader access to evidence encompassing art and architecture, documentary and literary sources, scientific texts and zooarchaeology; finally, longer academic studies engage with and advance the field. The series promotes work that challenges preconceptions, advances the field of study, and engages a wide readership.

Diane Heath and Victoria Blud
Series editors

CONTENTS

Preface	xi
List of illustrations	xiii
Introduction	1
The Dragon and Medieval Scholarship	15
The Dragon and Medieval Religion	35
The Medieval Dragon and Folklore	63
The Dragon and Medieval Literature	81
Outlook and Conclusion	115
Endnotes	121
Further reading	151
Bibliography	155
Index	167

PREFACE

THIS SHORT STUDY has many fathers. My fascination with dragons goes back several decades and probably started with the dragon Smaug in *The Hobbit* (the book version, and not his rather embarrassingly dim-witted counterpart in the movie), grew further upon encountering the dragons of medieval literature, such as the *Beowulf* dragon, and found unexpected food for thought with the dragon-lore of central Switzerland (especially Lucerne). All these aspects are reflected, one way or another, in the following pages.

I also owe a great debt to a multitude of people – scholars, fellow dragonologists and laypeople alike – who discussed dragon matters with me, read parts of my text in various draft forms, provided feedback and inspiration, or contributed to the publication of the book in some other way. In alphabetical order, I would like to thank: Martin Arnold, Anke Eissmann (who provided the illustrations), Jennifer Fellows, Lynn Forest-Hill, Diane Heath (for inviting me to contribute to this new series), Sarah Lewis (University of Wales Press), Sophia Mehlhausen, Paul Michel, Allan

Turner, Paul Wackers, and the anonymous peer-reviewer at University of Wales Press. Needless to say, any remaining mistakes and the interpretations and opinions expressed are ultimately my own.

I hope that my study will inspire readers to explore further this fascinating beast.

Jena on the Saale, January 2019
Thomas Honegger

LIST OF ILLUSTRATIONS

Frontispiece: Dragon. vi

Illustration 1: The dragon and the hoard. 4

Illustration 2: The different types of the Western dragon. 9

Illustration 3: Illustration showing the different types of dragons from Edward Topsell's *The History of Four-footed Beasts and Serpents* (1658 edn) for the chapter 'Of the dragon' (p. 701). 21

Illustration 4: Dragon binding an elephant. Based on an illustration from a thirteenth-century English bestiary (London, British Library, MS Harley 4751, fol. 58v). 28

Illustration 5: Saint Michael fighting the devil-dragon. Based on Martin Schongauer's *Saint Michael fighting the dragon* (1480–90). 38

Illustration 6: Saint George fighting the dragon. Based on Vittore Carpaccio's (1465–1526) *St George and the Dragon* (1502). 44

Illustration 7: Saint George fighting the dragon on a recruitment poster during the First World War. Based on poster no. 108 issued by the Parliamentary Recruiting Committee in 1915. 49
Illustration 8: Saint Margaret bursting from the dragon's belly. Based on an illustration in a fifteenth-century Book of Hours (Belgium, *c.*1440; New York, Morgan Library, MS M.19, fol. 157v). 51
Illustration 9: Jaws of hell. Based on a stained-glass window in Bourges Cathedral (twelfth century). 53
Illustration 10: The Woman of the Apocalypse. Based on a mid-thirteenth-century manuscript illustration (New York, Morgan Library, MS M.524, fol. 8v). 55
Illustration 11: 'Mondsichelmadonna'. Based on Geertgen tot Sint Jans's (AD *c.*1460–*c.*1490) *The Glorification of the Virgin* (*c.*1480). 57
Illustration 12: Chasuble with Chinese silks depicting dragons. Lucerne (Switzerland) *c.*1400. 58
Illustration 13: A young wyvern. 71
Illustration 14: Beowulf fighting the dragon. 91
Illustration 15: Bevis fighting the dragon of Cologne. 104

TABLES

Table 1: The table of the animal kingdom in Carolus Linnaeus's first edition (1735) of *Regnum Animale*. 18

EXTENSIVE QUOTES AND ILLUSTRATIONS

The modern English translation of *Bevis of Hampton* used (by permission of the author) is by Lynn Forest-Hill, *Bevis of Hampton* (Southampton: So: To Speak/Southampton Festivals, in association with Gumbo Press, 2015).

The edition and modern English translation of *Beowulf* used (by permission of the author) is by Benjamin Slade, *Beowulf: Diacritically Marked Text and Facing Translation*, *http://www.heorot.dk/beo-intro-rede.html*, 2002–12 (accessed 25 August 2018).

INTRODUCTION

Ðá se gæst ongan glédum spíwan,
beorht hofu bærnan· bryneléoma stód
eldum on andan· nó ðaér áht cwices
láð lyftfloga laéfan wolde·

Then the demon began to spew flames,
to burn bright houses; the gleam of fire rose
to the horror of the men; nor there anything alive
the hateful air-flier wished to leave;
(*Beowulf*, lines 2312–15)[1]

THE EARLIEST ATTESTED dragon in medieval English literature makes his debut in style by wreaking fiery havoc from the skies on the unsuspecting inhabitants of Geatland in southern Sweden. The sudden attack is due to the fact that the dragon's centuries-long repose has been disturbed by a fugitive serf who steals a golden cup from the dragon's hoard to appease the anger of his master. This theft, however, arouses the wrath of the dragon, who scours the landscape in search of the thief and burns homes, villages and even the great hall of Beowulf, their king. The Old English poem then continues to relate the

hoary warrior-king's last fight against the monstrous foe to save his people and to rid the land of this menace. He and his nephew Wiglaf succeed in killing the dragon, yet shortly afterwards Beowulf succumbs to the poison spreading from the wound he contracted during the battle.

The *Beowulf* dragon is not only one of the earliest medieval dragons, but also one of the most typical ones. It has wings and is able to fly, breathes fire, jealously guards a hoard inside a barrow, can only be killed by a well-aimed thrust at its unprotected underside, and its bite is poisonous. These are all features that most modern

readers associate with the prototypical medieval dragon, yet whose combined occurrence is very rare in actual medieval texts. The Old English *Maxims* II, for example, sees the guarding of a hoard inside a barrow as the defining feature of the dragon and does not mention any of the other characteristics:

> Draca sceal on hlæwe, / frod, frætwum wlanc.
> A dragon must live in a barrow, / old and proud of
> his treasures.
> (*Maxims* II, lines 26b–7a)[2]

Illustration 1:
The dragon and the hoard. Drawing by Anke Eissmann.

Fafnir, probably the most famous dragon of Germanic legend, shares this key element, and it was actually due to the acquisition of the ill-gotten treasure that the dwarf Fafnir turned into a dragon. He spends most of his time jealously guarding his hoard and Sigurd/Siegfried is able to kill him only once he finds a way to get at Fafnir's unprotected underbelly. Yet though Fafnir exhibits at least two of the typical characteristics of a dragon, he has neither wings nor does he breathe fire but seems to 'blow poison' instead.[3]

In the original text, Fafnir is referred to by the Old Norse *ormr*, which translates as serpent or dragon. It is a word with cognates in most Indo-European languages, such as Latin *vermis*, Old Russian *vermije*, Germanic **wurmiz*, Old High German *wurm*, Old English *wyrm*, etc. All these words seem to go back to an Indo-European root **wr̥mi-* 'worm', which is in turn derived from the Indo-European root *wer-*[2] 'to turn, to bend'. The *Beowulf* dragon, too, is called *wyrm*, which the poet uses next to *draca*, a loanword from Latin *draco*, that, in turn, derives from Greek *drakon*. The poet uses them as full synonyms, much as Modern German still has *Lindwurm* and *Drache* to refer to one and the same monster. This seemingly indiscriminate use of different terms for one and the same creature illustrates an important difference between poets and scholars. The former show little concern about the potential zoological implications of the different terms and focus almost exclusively on the function of the monster within the narrative. As a consequence, the 'monstrous terminology' of medieval literature remains rather vague and though there seem to exist certain differentiations, they are hard to reconstruct. Take, for example, the following description from the Old English poem *Beowulf*. The Geats who had followed the track of Grendel's mother come to a mere and see the following:

> gesáwon ðá æfter wætere *wyrmcynnes* fela
> sellice *saédracan* sund cunnian,
> swylce on næshleoðum *nicras* licgean
> ðá on undernmaél oft bewitigað
> sorhfulne síð on seglráde,
> *wyrmas* ond *wildéor*·
>
> they saw then through the water many *of the race of serpents*,
> strange *sea-dragon*[s] exploring the lake,
> also on the cape-slopes were lounging *nicors*,
> they in mid-morning often carry out
> grievous sorties on the sail-road,
> *serpents* and *wild beasts*;[4]
> (*Beowulf*, lines 1425–30a; italics mine)

Without intending to undertake an analysis of the various expressions comprising the semantic field of 'monstrous animals'[5] in this passage, it becomes clear that the *sædracan* (acc. pl. of *sædraca*) mentioned do not belong to the same category as the imposing *draca/wyrm* of the second part of the poem. The *sædracan* are, together with the *nicras*, smaller-scale sea-monsters that are dealt with by the hero almost by the dozen.[6]

The *Beowulf* passage highlights one of the crucial points of a semasiological approach:[7] the same term, here *draca*, is used for sometimes widely differing creatures, and the context is often not sufficient to establish the exact meaning of the word or to determine the nature of the creature we are talking about. It is very rare to find medieval scholars as obliging as the unknown

Old English glossator who elucidates the Old English term *hron* by setting it into relation to other marine animals:

> Manducat unumquodque animal in mari alterum. Et dicunt quod vii minoribus saturantur maiores. ut vii fiscas sélaes fyllu, sifu sélas hronaes fyllu, sifu hronas hualaes fyllu.[8]
>
> Latin text: In the sea one creature devours another. It is said that seven smaller ones are sufficient to satisfy the appetite of the bigger ones.
> Old English text: Seven fishes are sufficient to satisfy a seal, seven seals are sufficient to satisfy a *hron*, and seven *hronas* are sufficient to satisfy a whale.

The gloss helps us to define more closely the animal referred to as *hron* (presumably a porpoise) as being in size somewhere in between the seal and the whale. Unfortunately, we have no similar gloss to elucidate the *sædracan* in *Beowulf* and the question of what kind of creatures they are exactly will probably remain a mystery forever.

This (from a linguistic point of view) deplorable semantic vagueness of poetic texts is mainly due to the fact that the main function of the *nicras* and *sædracan* is to constitute a challenge or obstacle to the hero's progress.[9] The audience is not very likely to show an interest in the finer points of the zoological categorization of the monster that is about to devour the hero, and therefore much is left to the imagination.[10]

This vagueness is not limited to poetic or fictional texts only but seems indissolubly connected with the Western dragon's very wide range of phenotypes,[11] which poses a challenge of its own to scientifically-minded dragonologists.

Illustration 2 shows some of the most frequent forms of Western dragons: among others, it depicts different types of the basilisk (a and g), the (Komodo) lizard dragon type (b), the wyvern (d and h) and the 'common' winged dragon (e and f).

Illustration 2: *The different types of* Western *dragon. Drawing by Anke* Eiss*mann*.

This diversity in shapes and forms seems to be a phenomenon found only in the Western cultural realm, whereas the Chinese dragon is characterized by an astonishing stability of its phenotype.[12] As we will see, not even the medieval scholars' attempts at systematization brought clarity to the matter[13] and the Western dragons' incompatibility with Carolus Linnaeus's (1707–78) scientific categories dealt them their death blow.

Although the phenotype of the dragon would differ from culture to culture and from one age to the next, the conceptual core of the dragon as a powerful, awe-inspiring and potentially dangerous being seems a universal element found in almost all human cultures. Theories explaining this phenomenon range from the nonsensical and fanciful to the plausible, and though we can disprove some of them, we cannot find conclusive evidence for the others. The following list presents some of the most popular ones:[14]

a) Dragons are the product of the early humans' confrontation with three dangerous animals: the big cat, the bird of prey and the snake.[15] David Jones, for example, argues that these three were synthesized into the neurobiological shorthand 'dragon'. Thus if early humans encountered anything with claws, fangs or a reptile body, they would not waste any time analysing and categorizing the creature but flee immediately.

b) Dragons are personifications of natural phenomena, such as volcanoes, thunder and lightning, whirlwinds, rainbows, etc. This theory helps to explain some of the culture-specific characteristics of the dragons, e.g. why some dragons are associated with rain and clouds while others are linked to fire.

c) Dragons are re-interpretations of reports about big reptiles such as crocodiles, big snakes such as pythons and anacondas, or Komodo dragons. This theory has its precursor in the medieval encyclopaedic tradition that starts with Isidore of Seville (AD c.560–636), who writes that the 'dragon (*draco*) is the largest of all the snakes, or of all the animals on earth'.[16]

d) Dragons are attempts to explain such puzzling finds as the fossilized bones or skeletons of dinosaurs.[17]

e) Dragons are re-interpretations of reports about encounters with dinosaurs that survived in secluded areas. This theory has its most popular variant in the 'Loch Ness Monster' phenomenon and is implicit in movies such as *The Lost World*, *King Kong* or *Godzilla* where dinosaurs are not only shown as having survived in out-of-the-way places, but also take over the narrative function of dragons.[18]

f) Dragons are genetically transmitted memories of the earliest mammals (resembling modern-day shrews or mice) whose existence overlapped with that of the dinosaurs. This theory assumes that mammals possess a hereditary memory; that is, they are able to pass on memories genetically over generations. This assumption is yet not scientifically proven and most scholars, as a consequence, reject this explanation as untenable.

The list could be continued yet would add little to the purpose of this book. Suffice it to say that the idea or concept of the dragon has been part of our evolutionary development and is most likely hard-wired into our brains. In the following paragraphs I'm going to sketch briefly the relevant pre-history of the medieval dragon and discuss some of the most formative dragon-figures, not only in the culture of Greek and Roman antiquity, but also in those of the Middle and Near East, which are more distant but nevertheless important for the biblical tradition.

Babylonian mythology presents Tiamat as a mighty being who is linked to the realm of salt water and who threatens to overthrow the young gods with an army of monsters. She is killed by Marduk, and from her two halves the earth and the sky are created. Structural parallels to later mythologies such as the Greek Olympians' struggle with the Titans[19] or the Germanic Aesir's fight against the giant Ymir are obvious, but we also notice echoes of the conflict between the sky-god Marduk and the ocean-goddess Tiamat in the biblical allusions to the antagonism between Yahwe and Leviathan.[20] Tiamat, like Leviathan, represents an aspect of the primordial chaos that has to be made subject to the ordering principle (here the sky god Marduk) and whose resources have to be harnessed for the creation of the cosmos in the meaning of 'an ordered whole'. This antagonism between an older, often chthonic or aquatic being (monster or god/goddess) and a representative of the new order (the culture hero) constitutes a pattern that is found in most of the later dragon stories, though often changed and adapted. We encounter it in Norse mythology in the antagonism between Thor and the Midgard Serpent

(Jörmungandr), in Classical myth in the conflict between the Greek Zeus and Typhon, or again in Apollo killing the Python. It also features in foundation myths that contain the defeat of a monster prior to the establishment of a new settlement, as for example in the story about the foundation of the city of Thebes by Cadmus, who slays the dragon guarding the Ismenian spring and thus ensures safe access to the essential water supply for his new city. The motif also travels down the centuries into the Christian era where, as we will see later on, it influences the depiction of the confrontations between saints as the bringers of the new doctrine of redemption and the dragons as the representatives of (native) pagan cults.

These later texts often lack the universal cosmological quality found in the earlier myths but represent the conflict as a more localized event. In addition, the dragons are now used as narrative elements in their own right, guarding treasure and special objects, and thus function as obstacles that have to be overcome by the hero on his quest. Typical representatives of this type would be the dragon Ladon with a hundred heads who watches over the golden apples growing in the Garden of the Hesperides, or the never-sleeping dragon who helps guard the Golden Fleece. These dragons, much more than their mythological-cosmic counterparts, exhibit close functional and symbolic parallels to the hoard-guarding dragons of the later Germanic tradition we met at the beginning of this chapter.

THE DRAGON AND MEDIEVAL SCHOLARSHIP

IN 1735 THE GREAT Swedish naturalist Carolus Linnaeus (1707–78) published the first edition of his *Regnum Animale*, in which he attempted a systematic taxonomy of the animal world. Below the 'Amphibia', which constitute the third column of his overview table of the animal world (table 1), he inserts a list entitled 'Paradoxa', a category Linnaeus created to accommodate all those creatures that defy classification and stand in opposition to his taxonomical endeavours.

It features, among others, the hydra, the unicorn ('monoceros veterum'), the satyr, the pelican in her piety who revives her young with her own blood, the phoenix and also the dragon ('draco'). They all pose a problem in as much as either their behaviour or their composite physical nature is in conflict with Linnaeus's taxonomic categories. In the second edition (1740), Linnaeus abandoned the ragbag category of 'paradoxa' where the dragons could have found a place in this brave new world of taxonomical rigour. This meant that the dragons were finally banished from the domain of natural science where, for more than a thousand years, they had led a more or less unproblematic existence as part of the family of the serpents. A little more than a

CAROLI LINNÆI

I. QUADRUPEDIA. *Corpus hirsutum. Pedes quatuor. Feminæ viviparæ, lactiferæ.*	II. AVES. *Corpus plumosum. Alæ duæ. Pedes duo. Rostrum osseum. Feminæ oviparæ.*	III. AMPHIBI[A]. *Corpus nudum, vel squamosum. Dentes* [illegible] *nulli: reliqui semper. Pinnæ null*[æ]
ANTHROPOMORPHA: Homo. Simia. Bradypus.	ACCIPITRES: Psittacus. Strix. Falco.	SERPENTIA: Testudo. *Corpus quadrupedium, caudatum, testa munitum.* Rana. *Corpus quadrupedium, cauda destitutum, squamis carens.* Lacerta. *Corpus quadrupedium, caudatum, squamosum.* Anguis. *Corpus apodum, teres, squamosum.*
FERÆ: Ursus. Leo. Tigris. Felis. Mustela. Didelphis. Lutra. Odobenus. Phoca. Hyæna. Canis. Meles. Talpa. Erinaceus. Vespertilio.	PICÆ: Paradisea. Coracias. Corvus. Cuculus. Picus. Certhia. Sitta. Upupa. Ispida.	
GLIRES: Hystrix. Sciurus. Castor. Mus. Lepus. Sorex.	MACRORHYNCHÆ: Grus. Ciconia. Ardea.	
JUMENTA: Equus. Hippopotamus. Elephas. Sus.	ANSERES: Platalea. Pelecanus. Cygnus. Anas. Mergus. Graculus. Colymbus. Larus.	
PECORA: Camelus. Cervus. Capra. Ovis. Bos.	SCOLOPACES: Hæmatopus. Charadrius. Vanellus. Tringa. Numenius. Fulica.	
	GALLINÆ: Struthio. Casuarius. Otis. Pavo. Meleagris. Gallina. Tetrao.	
	PASSERES: Columba. Turdus. Sturnus. Alauda. Motacilla. Luscinia. Parus. Hirundo. Loxia. Ampelis. Fringilla.	
Ordines. Genera. Characteres Generum. Species.		

AMPHIBIORUM Classem ulterius continuare noluit [illegible] tas Creatoris; Ea enim si tot Generibus, quot reliq[uorum a]nimalium Classes comprehendunt, gauderet; vel si v[era essent] quæ de Draconibus, Basiliscis, ac ejusmodi mo[nstris] τεράτολόγοι fabulantur, certè humanum genus terra[m inhabi]tare vix posset.

PARADOXA

HYDRA corpore anguino, pedibus duobus, [illegible] pem, & totidem capitibus, alarum expers, asservat[ur Ham]burgi, similitudinem referens Hydræ Apocalypsis [Johan]NIS CAP. XII. & XIII. descriptæ. Eaque tanquam [verè a]nimalis speciem plurimis præbuit, sed falsò. Natura [sibi sem]per similis plura capita in uno corpore nunquam pro[duxit na]turaliter. Fraudem & artificium, cum ipsi vidimus, [den]tes Ferino-mustelini, ab Amphibiorum dentibus div[ersi] cillime detexerunt.

RANA-PISCIS s. RANÆ IN PISCEM METAMO[RPHOSIS] valdè paradoxa est, quum Natura mutationem Gene[ris unius] in aliam diversæ Classis non admittat. Ranæ, ut A[mphibia] omnia, pulmonibus gaudent & ossibus spinosis. P[isces spi]nosi, loco pulmonum, branchiis instruuntur. E[rgo legi] Naturæ contraria foret hæc mutatio. Si enim pisc[is] structus est branchiis, erit diversus à Rana & Amph[ibiis; si] verò pulmone, erit Lacerta: nam toto cœlo à Cho[ndrop]terygiis & Plagiuris differt.

MONOCEROS *Veterum*, corpore equino, pedibu[s] cornu recto, longo, spiraliter intorto, Pictorum [inven]tum est. MONODON *Artedi* ejusmodi cornu gerit, verò partibus multum differt.

PELECANUS rostro vulnus infligens femori suo, [profluen]te sanguine sitim pullorum levet, fabulosè ab Li[bris tra]ditur. Ansam fabulæ dedit saccus sub gula pendulus.

SATYRUS caudatus, hirsutus, barbatus, huma[num] ferens corpus, gesticulationibus valde deditus, salac[issimus] Simiæ species est, si unquam aliquis visus fuit. *Homi*[nes] que *Caudati*, de quibus recentiores peregrinatores mu[lta nar]rant, ejusdem generis sunt.

BOROMETZ s. AGNUS SCYTHICUS plantis accense[tur] agno assimilatur; cui caulis e terra plantæ è terra pens umbilicum intrat; idemque sanguine prædicu[s à lupis] devorari temerè dicitur. Est autem artificiosè ex r[adicibus] Filicinis Americanis compositus. Naturaliter autem [illegible] *brys Ovis* allegoricè descriptus, qui omnia data hab[et at]bus.

PHOENIX, Avis species, cujus unicum in mundo [indivi]duum, & quæ decrepita ex ferali busto, quod sibi [ex aro]matibus struxerat, repuerascere fabulosè fertur, felicem [vi]tam prioris vitæ periodum. Est verò PALMA DACT[YLIFE]RA. vid. *Kæmpf*.

BERNICLA s. ANSER SCOTICUS & CONCHA ANAT[IFERA] è lignis putridis in mare abjectis nasci à Veteribus c[reditur]. Sed fucum imposuit *Lepas* internaneis suis penniformi[bus eo] modo adhærentibus, quasi verus ille anser *Bernicla* ind[ica]tur.

DRACO corpore anguino, duobus pedibus, duab[us alis] Vespertilionis instar, est *Lacerta alata*, vel *Raja* pe[r artem] monstrosè ficta, & siccata.

AUTOMA MORTIS Horologii minimi sonitum edens [in pa]rietibus, est *Pediculus pulsatorius* dictus, qui ligna p[utrida] eaque inhabitat.

Table 1: *The table of the animal kingdom in Carolus Linnaeus's first edition* (1735) *of* Regnum Animale.[3]

REGNUM ANIMALE.

V PISCES.

r apodum, pinnis veris instructum, nudum, vel squamosum.

Genus	Character	Species
Thrichechus.	Dentes in utroque maxilla. Dorsum impenne.	Manatus. Vacca mar.
Catodon.	Dentes in inferiore maxilla. Dorsum impenne.	Cet. Fistula in rostro. Art. Cete Clus.
Monodon.	Dens in superiore max. 2. Dorsum impenne.	Monoceros. Unicorn.
Balaena.	Dentes in sup. max. cornei. Dorsum saepius impenne.	B. Groenland. B. Finfisch. B. Maxill. inf. latiore. Art.
Delphinus.	Dentes in utroque maxilla. Dorsum pinnatum.	Orcha. Delphinus. Phocaena.
Raja.	Foramina branch. utrinq. 5. Corpus depressum.	Raja clav. asp. laev. &c. Squatino-Raja. Altavela. Pastinaca mar. Aquila. Torpedo. Bos Ve.
Squalus.	Foram. branch. utrinq. 5. Corpus oblongum.	Lamia. Galeus. Canicula. Vulpes mar. Zygaena. Squatina. Centrina. Pristis.
Acipenser.	Foram. branch. utrinq. 1. Os edentul. tubulatum.	Sturio. Huso. Ichthyocolla.
Petromyzon.	Foram. branch. utrinq. 7. Corpus bipenne.	[illegible] Lampetra. Mustela.
Lophius.	Caput magnitudine corporis. Appendices horizontaliter [illegible] ambientes.	Rana piscatrix. Guacucuja.
Cyclopterus.	Pinnae ventrales in unicam circularem concretae.	Lumpus. Lepus mar.
Ostracion.	Pinna ventralis nulla. Cutis dura, saepe aculeata.	Orbis div. sp. Pisc. triangul. Atinga. Hystrix. Ostracion. Lagocephalus.
Balistes.	Dentes contigui maximi. Aculei aliquot robusti in dorso.	Guaperua. Halvis. Capriscus. Caper.
Gasterosteus.	Membr. branch. ossicula 3. Pinnae [illegible]	Aculeatus. Spinachia. Pungitius.
Zeus.	Corpus compressum. Squama [illegible]	Aper. Faber. Gallus mar.
Cottus.	Membrana branch. ossic. 6. Caput aculeatum, corpore latius.	Cataphractus. Scorpio mar. Cottus. Gobio fl. capit.
Trigla.	Appendices ad pinn. pect. articulatae 2 vel 3.	Lyra. Gurnardus. Cuculus. Lucerna. Hirundo. Milvus. Mullus barb. & imberb.
Trachinus.	Operculo branch. aculeata. Oculi vicini in vertice.	Draco. Araneus mar. Uranoscopus.
Perca.	Membr. branch. ossicul. 7. Pinnae dorsales 1 vel 2.	Perca. Lucioperca. Cernua. Schraitser.
Sparus.	Operculo branch. squamosa. Labia dentes tegunt. Dentes molares obtusi.	Salpa. Melanurus. Sparus. Sargus. Chromis. Mormyrus. Maena. Smaris. Boops. Dentex. Erythrinus. Pagrus. Aurata. Cantharus.
Labrus.	Labia crassa dentes teg. Color speciosus.	Julis. Sachettus. Turdus diversar. species.
Mugil.	Membr. branch. ossic. 6. Caput totum squamosum.	Mugil. Cephalus.
Scomber.	Membr. branch. ossic. 7. Pinna dorsi 2 vel plures.	Glaucus. Amia. Scomber. Thynnus. Trachurus. Saurus.
Xiphias.	Rostrum apice ensiforme. Pinnae ventrales nullae.	Gladius.
Gobius.	Pinnae vent. in 1 simpl. concr. Squama aspera.	Gob. niger. Jozo. Paganellus. Aphya.
Gymnotus.	Membr. branch. ossicul. 5. Pinna dorsalis nulla.	Carapo.
Muraena.	Membr. branch. ossic. 10. Tubuli in apice rostri. 2.	Anguilla. Conger. Flota. Serpens mar.
Blennus.	Pinnae ventr. constant ossic. 2. Caput admodum declive.	Alauda non crist. & crist. Blennus. Gattorugine.
Gadus.	Membr. branch. ossic. 7. Pinnae dorsi 2 vel 3.	Asellus diversar. species. Merluccius. Anthias. Mustela. Egrefinus.
Pleuronectes.	Membr. branch. oss. 6. Oculi ambo in eodem latere.	Rhombus diversar. species. Passer. Limanda. Hippoglossus. Bugloss. Solea.
Ammodytes.	Membr. branch. ossic. 7. Pinna ventr. nulla.	Ammodytes. Tobianus.
Coryphaena.	Membr. branch. ossic. 5. Pinna dorsi a capite ad caudam.	Hippurus. Pompilus. Novacula. Psetta.
Echeneis.	Striis transversis, asperis, in superna capitis parte.	Remora.
Esox.	Membr. branch. ossic. 14.	Lucius. Belone. Acus maxima squamosa.
Salmo.	Membr. branch. ossic. 10–12. Corpus maculosum.	Salmo. Trutta. Umbla. Carpio lacustr.
Osmerus.	Membr. branch. ossic. 7–8. Dentes in max. lingu. palat.	Eperlanus. Spirinchus. Saurus.
Coregonus.	Membr. branch. ossic. 8–10. Appendix pinniformis.	Albula. Lavaretus. Thymallus. Oxyrhynchus.
Clupea.	Membr. branch. ossic. 8. Venter acutus serratus.	Harengus. Sprattus. Encrasicholus. Alosa.
Cyprinus.	Membr. branch. ossic. 3. Dentes ad orificium ventriculi tantum.	Erythrophthal. Mugil. fluv. Brama. Ballerus. Capito. Nasus. A. M. Carassius. Cypr. nobilis. Tinca. Barbus. Rutilus. Alburnus. Leuciscus. Phoxinus. Gobius fl.
Cobitis.	Caput compressum. Pinna dorsi & ventrales eidem a rostro distantes.	Cobitis. Barbatula. Misgurn.
Syngnathus.	Opercula branch. ex laminis 3. Maxilla a lateribus clausa.	Acus lumbr. Acus Aristot. Hippocampus.

V. INSECTA.

Corpus crusta ossea cutis loco tectum. *Caput* antennis instructum.

Order	Genus	Character	Species
COLEOPTERA. *Alae* elytris duobus tectae.	Blatta.	§. Pedes externa facile distinc. *Elytra* concreta. *Alae* nullae. *Antennae* truncatae.	Scarab. tardipes. Blatta foetida.
	Dytiscus.	*Pedes* postici remorum forma & usu. *Ant.* setaceae. *Sterni* apex bifurcus.	Hydrocantharus. Scarab. aquaticus.
	Meloë.	*Elytra* mollia, flexilia, corpore breviora. *Ant.* moniliformes. Ex articulis oleum fundens.	Scarab. majalis. Scarab. unctuosus.
	Forficula.	*Elytra* brevissima, rigida. *Cauda* bifurca.	Staphylinus. Auricularia.
	Notopeda.	Pectum in dorso [illegible] *Ant.* capillaceae.	Scarab. elasticus.
	Mordella.	*Cauda* aculeo rigido simplici armata. *Ant.* setaceae, breves.	Negatur ab Aristotele.
	Curculio.	*Rostrum* productum, teres, simplex. *Ant.* clavatae in medio Rostri positae.	Curculio.
	Buprestis.	*Cornu* 1. simplex, rigidum, fixum. *Ant.* capitatae, foliosae.	Rhinoceros. Scarab. monoceros.
	Lucanus.	*Cornua* 2. ramosa, rigida, mobilia. *Ant.* capitatae, foliaceae.	Cervus volans.
	Scarabaeus.	§. Antennae truncatae. *Ant.* clavatae foliaceae. *Cornua* nulla.	Scarab. pilularis. Melolontha. Dermestes.
	Dermestes.	*Ant.* clavatae horizontaliter perfoliatae. *Clypeus* planiusculus, emarginatus.	Cantharus fasciatus.
	Cassida.	*Ant.* clavato-fusiformes. *Clypeus* planus, antice rotundatus.	Scarab. clypeatus.
	Chrysomela.	*Ant.* simplices, clypeo longiores. *Corpus* subrotundum.	Cantharellus.
	Coccionella.	*Ant.* simplices, brevissimae. *Corpus* hemisphaericum.	Cochinella vulg.
	Gyrinus.	*Ant.* simplices. *Corpus* breve. *Pedibus* posticis saltans.	Pulex aquaticus. Pulex plantarum.
	Necydalis.	*Ant.* clavato-productae. *Clypeus* angustus, rotundatus.	Scarabaeo-formica.
	Attalabus.	*Ant.* simplices, constructae articulis orbicularibus, praeter ultim. globosum.	Scarab. praerosus.
	Cantharis.	§. Antennae Setaceae. *Clypeus* planus, margine undique prominente. *Elytra* flexilia.	Cantharis offic.
	Carabus.	*Clypeus* fere planus, marg. prominente. *Elytra* fragilia.	Cantharus foetidus. Cantharellus auratus.
	Cicindela.	*Clypeus* cylindraceus vel teres. *Forceps* oris prominens.	Cantharus Marianus.
	Leptura.	*Clypeus* subrotundus. *Pedes* longi. *Corpus* tenue acuminatum.	Scarab. taurus.
	Cerambyx.	*Clypeus* ad latera mucrone prominens. *Ant.* corpus longitudine aequant, vel superant.	Capricornus.
	Buprestis.	*Clypeus* superne a pendice elevatus notatus.	Scarab. sylvaticus.
ANGIOPTERA. *Alae* omnibus datae, elytris destitutae.	Papilio.	*Rostrum* spirale. *Alae* 4.	Papilio alis erectis. Psyche — planis. Phalaena — compressis.
	Libellula.	*Cauda* foliosa. *Alae* 4. expansae.	Perla. Virgunculа.
	Ephemera.	*Cauda* setosa. *Alae* 4. erectae.	Musca Ephemera.
	Hemerobius.	*Cauda* setosa. *Alae* 4. compressae.	Phryganea.
	Panorpa.	*Cauda* cheliformis. *Alae* 4. *Rostr.* corn.	Musca scorpiurus.
	Raphidia.	*Cauda* spinoso-setacea. *Alae* 4. *Cap.* corn.	Non descripta.
	Apis.	*Cauda* aculeo simplici. *Alae* 4.	Crabro. Vespa. Bombylius. Apis.
	Ichneumon.	*Cauda* aculeo partito. *Alae* 4.	Ichneumon. Musca tripilis.
	Musca.	*Stylus* sub alis capitatus. *Alae* 2.	Muscae div. spec. Oestrum Vet. Oestrum Lapponum. Tabanus. Culex. Teredo nav. Tipula. Formica-leo.
HEMIPTERA. *Alae* elytris destitutae, Quibusdam tantum individuis concessae.	Gryllus.	*Pedes* 6. *Alae* 4. *superiores* crassiores.	Gryllus domesticus. Gryllo-talpa. Locusta. Mantis.
	Lampyris.	*Pedes* 6. *Clypeus* planus. *Alae* 4.	Cicindela.
	Formica.	*Pedes* 6. *Alae* 4. *Cauda* aculeata condit.	Formica.
	Cimex.	*Pedes* 6. *Alae* 4. cruciferae. *Rostrum* subulatum, rectum.	Cimex lectularius. Orsodachne. Tipula aquatica. Bruchus.
	Notonecta.	*Pedes* 6. quorum postici remorum figura & usu. *Alae* 4. cruciferae.	Notonecta aquatica.
	Nepa.	*Pedes* 4. *Frons* chelifera. *Al.* 4. crucif.	Scorpio aquat.
	Scorpio.	*Pedes* 8. *Frons* chelifera, aculeata. *Alae* 4. [illegible]	Scorpio terrestris.
APTERA. *Alae* nullae.	Pediculus.	*Pedes* 6. *Antennae* capite breviores.	Pediculus humanus. Ped. avium. Ped. piscium. Ped. pulsatorius.
	Pulex.	*Pedes* 6. saltatrices.	Pulex vulgaris.
	Monoculus.	*Pes* 1.? *Antennae* bifidae.	Pulex arborescens Swam. Monoculus Brasil. Apus Frisch.
	Acarus.	*Pedes* 8. articulis 3 constantes. *Oculi* 2. *Ant.* minimae.	Ricinus. Scorpio-araneus. Pedic. inguinalis. Pedic. Scarabaei. Pedic. avium. Araneus coccineus.
	Araneus.	*Pedes* 8. *Oculi* communiter 8.	Araneus. Tarantula. Phalangium.
	Cancer.	*Pedes* 12. *priores* cheliformes.	Cancer. Astacus. Pagurus. Squilla. Maja. Eremita. Gammarus.
	Oniscus.	*Pedes* 14.	Asellus officin. Asellus aquat.
	Scolopendria.	*Pedes* 20. & ultra.	Scolop. terrestris. Scolop. marina. Julus.

VI. VERMES.

Corporis *Musculi* ab una parte basi cuidam solidae affixi.

Order	Genus	Character	Species
REPTILIA. Nuda, artubus destituta.	Gordius.	*Corpus* filiforme, teres, simplex.	Seta aquatica. Vena Medina.
	Taenia.	*Corpus* fasciatum, planum, articulatum.	Lumbricus longus.
	Lumbricus.	*Corpus* teres, annulo prominenti cinctum.	Lumbricus terrestris. Lumbricus latus. Ascaris.
	Hirudo.	*Corpus* inferne planum, superne convex. tentaculis destitutum.	Sanguisuga.
	Limax.	*Corpus* inferne planum, superne conv. tentaculis instructum.	Limax.
TESTACEA. Habitaculo Lapideo instructa.	Cochlea.	*Testa* univalvis, spiralis, unilocularis.	Helix. Labyrinthus. Voluta. Cochlea [illegible] Buccinum. Lyra. Turbo. Cassida. Strombus. Fistula. Terebellum. Murex. Purpura. Aporrhais. Nerita. Trochus.
	Nautilus.	*Testa* univalvis, spiralis, multilocularis.	Nautilus. Orthoceros. Lituus.
	Cypraea.	*Testa* univalvis, convoluta, rima longitudinali.	Concha Veneris. Porcellana.
	Haliotis.	*Testa* univalvis, patula, leviter concava, perforata, ad angulum spiralis.	Auris marina.
	Patella.	*Testa* univalvis, concava, simplex.	Patella.
	Dentalium.	*Testa* univalvis, teres, simplex.	Dentalium. Entalium. Tubus vermicul.
	Concha.	*Testa* bivalvis.	Mytulus. Valva [illegible] Pholas. Bucardium. Perna. Chama. Solenes. Tellina. Pinna. Ostrea. Pecten. Musculus. [illegible]
	Lepas.	*Testa* multivalvis. *Valvulis* duabus pluribus	Concha anatifera. Vermes tubulati. Balanus marinus.
ZOOPHYTA. Artubus donata.	Tethys.	*Corpus* forma variabile, molle, nudum.	Tethya. Holothurium. [illegible]
	Echinus.	*Corpus* subrotundum, testa tectum, aculeis armatum.	Echinus marinus.
	Asterias.	*Corpus* radiatum, corio tectum, scabrum.	Stella marina. Stella oligactis. St. pentadactyla. St. polydactyla.
	Medusa.	*Corpus* orbiculatum, gelatinosum, subtus filamentosum.	Urtica marina. Urt. vermiformis. Urt. crinita. Urt. [illegible]
	Sepia.	*Corpus* oblongum, interne osseum, anterius octo artubus donatum.	Sepia. Loligo.
	Microcosmus.	*Corpus* variis heterogeneis tectum.	Microcosmus marinus.

century before the publication of Linnaeus's *Regnum Animale*, the English scholar Edward Topsell (1572–1625) had, in his *The History of Serpents* (1608), still dedicated an entire chapter to the dragon (illustration 3).[1]

Topsell's encyclopaedia is based on the works by Conrad Gessner (1516–65) and Ulisse Aldrovandi (1522–1605) who, in turn, are the successors of medieval encyclopaedists such as Bartholomaeus Anglicus (*De*

proprietas rerum, after AD 1235), Thomas of Cantimpré (*Liber de natura rerum*, AD *c.*1240) or Vincent of Beauvais (*Speculum naturale*, AD *c.*1250–60).[2] Linnaeus's critical view of dragons is indicative of, and ultimately caused by, the paradigm shift in the European intellectual outlook that is characteristic of the Age of Enlightenment/Age of Reason. For centuries the entry ticket for an animal or any other creature into one of the big encyclopaedias of the Middle Ages was a reference

Illustration 3: *Illustration showing the different types of dragons from Edward Topsell's* The History of Four-footed Beasts and Serpents (1658 *edn*) *for the chapter 'Of the dragon'* (*p.* 701).

in the Bible or the works of one of the *auctores*, such as Aristotle or Pliny. The task of the scholar was then to find an explanation or interpretation for what the Bible and the *auctores* said. John Trevisa, in his 1399 translation of Bartholomaeus Anglicus's work, mentions the biblical texts twice in his introduction to Book XVIII ('De animalibus'). He writes that one of the aims of his work is to describe and discuss all the things and creatures of which 'mencioun is ymade in holy writte' and that are 'ynempned in tixt and in glose'.[4]

The encyclopaedists did not see their work as being opposed to the spiritual approach and the symbolic-allegorical interpretation of the world, but rather as part of a tradition that also comprises more explicitly exegetical-allegorical works such as the texts of the *Hexameron* tradition, the *Physiologus* and the various types of bestiaries. This exegetical tradition gives commentaries on and interpretations of the objects and animals mentioned in the Bible, found as for example in Homilies VII to IX of Ambrose's *Hexameron* (second half of the fourth century), which discuss the animals of the water, the air and the land within the context of the biblical six days of creation. The somewhat older *Physiologus*, which is assumed to have originated in Alexandria in the third century AD, is believed to have contained forty-nine chapters, of which forty-one deal with animals or mythical beings, six with stones (including the pearl) and two with trees. It was soon translated into Latin and thus found a wider audience for its allegorical view of creation. A typical chapter is headed by a quotation from the Scriptures, which either explicitly mentions the animal (or other subject) or can be linked to it in some other way. It then continues with a description of the subject's natural habits (the 'natura' part), which is followed by the allegorical interpretation of the characteristics mentioned (the 'significatio' part). To provide an example I quote part of the entry on the pelican, as given in T. H. White's *The Book of Beasts*:[5]

> The Pelican is excessively devoted to its children. But when these have been born and begin to grow up, they flap their parents in the face with their wings, and the parents, striking back, kill them. Three days afterward the mother pierces her breast, opens her side, and lays herself across her young, pouring out her blood over the dead bodies. This brings them to life again.
>
> In the same way, Our Lord Jesus Christ, who is the originator and maker of all created things, begets us and calls us into being out of nothing. We, on the contrary, strike him in the face . . . by devoting ourselves to the creation rather than the creator.
>
> That is why he ascended into the height of the cross, and, his side having been pierced, there came from it blood and water for our salvation and eternal life.[6]

This dual structure and the interpretation of the creation as *liber naturae* ('the Book of Nature') links the *Physiologus* chapters to the tradition of biblical exegesis on the one hand and, on the other, to the encyclopaedias.[7] It is the close connection with the latter that led to a significant increase of content in the twelfth century, when the original

number of chapters doubled. Most of these additions were taken from Isidore's *Etymologiae* and the enlarged versions became known as 'bestiaries'.

As T. H. White puts it: 'In the ages of faith, people believed that the Universe was governed by a controlling mind and was capable of a rational explanation. They believed that everything meant something.'[8] Thus, the focus was on the symbolic-spiritual meaning and not so much on the concrete object or creature itself. Indeed, one could say that, as soon as a thing or being or a quality thereof stood for a higher truth, its material existence became, for the exegete, relatively unimportant. Therefore, the spiritual truth provided the starting point for and basis of the allegorical interpretation of an object or being, or of one of its qualities. Yet the Book of Nature's credibility and authority were inferior to those of the divinely inspired Scriptures themselves. As a consequence, the Book of Nature might serve as a storehouse for illustrations of dogmatic truths, but it could never be used as the basis of an allegorical deduction of such a truth. Considering these basic differences between the two applications of the allegorical interpretation, it is all the more understandable, then, that the exegetes had to fall back on the only secure foundation when interpreting the Book of Nature, namely the spiritual truths of the Bible. Thus, the illustrations taken from natural history came to be based on the theologically solid groundwork of the Scriptures, and if the natural historical examples turned out to be wrong, it did not diminish the validity of the spiritual truths. This was what St Augustine implied in his often-quoted statement about the characteristics of 'the pelican in her piety' that is said to tear open her breast to revive her young with her blood. At the same time, we can observe the exegete's awareness of the possible difficulties that the allegorization of doubtful natural scientific information may have caused, and his efforts to anticipate them.

> These birds (the pelicans) are said to slay their young with blows of their beaks, and for three days to mourn them when slain by themselves in the nest: after which they say the mother wounds herself deeply, and pours forth her blood over her young, bathed in which they recover life. This may be true, it may be false: yet if it be true, see how it agrees with Him (Christ), who gave us life by His blood. It agrees with Him in that the mother's flesh recalls to life her young with her blood; it agrees well.[9]

Critical evaluation of traditional lore was thus possible,[10] yet it had as yet neither the importance nor the status it would acquire in the Age of Reason. And since the dragon was not only a creature well known from folklore and mythology but also from the works of both biblical scholars as well as *auctores*,[11] it took the profound change of the Enlightenment before its existence was seriously questioned.[12]

Above and beyond all the arguments outlined so far, we have some additional reasons why the dragon survived in the encyclopaedic tradition for such a long time. First, the criteria used by the encyclopaedists to categorize creatures were more flexible and they paid greater attention to what we would call 'accidental criteria'. Thus, to use a well-known example, a mammal such as the whale would traditionally be grouped with the fish because it lived in the water all the time. Furthermore, the encyclopaedists, true to their

name, strove for comprehensiveness rather than internal consistency and would therefore list unrelated or even contradictory pieces of information rather than omitting anything. In the case of the dragon, this tendency causes the entries to proliferate, which is mainly due to the Western dragon's widely diversified phenotype and different characteristics, as we will see later in this chapter.

Isidore of Seville (AD *c.*560–636), whose *Etymologiae* (AD *c.*625) constitute the link between the natural science knowledge of antiquity and that of the later Middle Ages, stands at the beginning of the medieval European encyclopaedic tradition. His chapter on the dragon (*draco*) has directly or indirectly been the starting point for most of the later encyclopaedia entries on the subject. He discusses the dragon in chapter IV ('De serpentibus', i.e. 'About snakes') in Book XII ('De animalibus') of his *Etymologiae*. Interestingly, in his general introduction to this chapter, he not only investigates the etymology of several terms used to denote snakes, but also observes that 'Snakes were always considered among the pagans as the spirits of places', which echoes the widespread function of the dragon (or large serpent) in pagan mythology and legend as the guardian of sacred places.[13] He also comments on the relationship between snakes and reptiles, arguing that not all reptiles are snakes, but that all snakes are reptiles. Thus, the snake

> crawls not with open steps but by tiny thrusts of its scales. But those animals that support themselves on four feet, like the lizard and the newt, are not snakes, but are called reptiles (*reptile*). Snakes are also reptiles, because they crawl (*repere*) on their stomach and breast. (p. 255)

This makes it clear that Isidore's inclusion of the dragon in his 'De serpentibus' chapter means that he is not talking about the four-legged (or even two-legged) dragon. Indeed, for Isidore the dragon is a very big snake, as he states explicitly in the opening of his description of his paragraph on the dragon:[14] 'The dragon (*draco*) is the largest of all the snakes, or of all the animals on earth' (p. 255).[15] Isidore goes on to talk about flying, which implies wings (*pace* Quetzalcoatl, the 'Feathered Serpent') that are, however, never explicitly mentioned and which stand in contrast to the explicit general theme, that is, the creeping and crawling of the snakes. He continues with his description as follows:

> It is crested, and has a small mouth and narrow pipes through which it draws breath and sticks out its tongue. It has its strength not in its teeth but in its tail, and it causes injury more by its lashing tail than with its jaws. (p. 255)

Isidore so far sticks to the pattern of giving a description that does not differ from the usual schema also used for other, less exotic or fantastic animal. He then addresses the question of poison and the dragon's enmity with the elephant (see illustration 4):

> Also, it does not harm with poison; poison is not needed for this animal to kill, because it kills whatever it wraps itself around. Even the elephant with his huge body is not safe from the dragon, for it lurks around the paths along which the elephants are accustomed to walk, and wraps around their legs in coils and kills them by suffocating them. It is born in Ethiopia and India in the fiery intensity of perpetual heat. (p. 255)

Illustration 4: *Dragon binding an elephant*. *Drawing by* Anke Eissmann *based on an illustration from a thirteenth-century* English *bestiary* (London, *British Library*, MS *Harley* 4751, *fol.* 58*v*).

In the first sentence, Isidore takes up the topic of poison mentioned in his introductory chapter on snakes, where he writes: 'Of these animals there are as many poisons as there are kinds, as many varieties of danger as there are of appearance, and as many causes of pain as there are colours' (p. 255). He does not claim that the dragon has no poison at all, but stresses the fact that it does not need it to kill even its biggest enemy, the elephant.[16] This enmity between dragon and elephant is already found in the authors of antiquity, such as Pliny the Elder (AD 23–79), who mentions it in Book VIII of his *Naturalis Historia*. The *Physiologus*, too, includes it in its chapter on the elephant[17] and the information thus found its way into the later bestiaries, with the dragon/snake symbolizing the Devil who tempted/attacked Adam and Eve (the elephants).[18] Isidore, however, does not include spiritual interpretations for any animals, he sticks to elucidating the meaning of the name and supplying 'facts'. Thus, Isidore does not link the rivalry between dragon and elephant to a spiritual dimension, and he also sticks to the 'facts' in all other cases mentioning the dragon – for example when he explains the origin of the red-coloured powder Cinnabar (p. 380), or when he refers to the enmity between the panther and the dragon (p. 251).[19] The dragon furthermore plays a role in the discussion of the *dracontites* (i.e. *dracontis*), a precious gemstone that has to be extracted from the brain of a living dragon (pp. 293, 326). Lastly, the dragon is part of India's exotic fauna (p. 286) and occurs in the stories pertaining to Greek mythology (p. 294).[20]

Things may sometimes get a bit too fantastic for modern tastes, yet Isidore remains clearly within the

limits of medieval science and there is no doubt that he presents the dragon as a real-world animal in its own right and posits it, as a member of the snake family, squarely within the zoological framework of late antiquity and the early Middle Ages.

Isidore's *Etymologiae* set the tone for the later encyclopaedias and it is therefore not surprising that our second representative text, John Trevisa's translation (AD 1399) of Bartholomaeus Anglicus's *De proprietas rerum* (after AD 1235), not only incorporates almost all the information from the *Etymologiae*, but also explicitly and repeatedly refers to Isidore as a source. Yet Trevisa also introduces some subtle changes as well as adding additional information from other sources (Solinus, Pliny, St Jerome and Aristotle).[21] I will therefore concentrate on those passages that deviate from and go beyond Isidore's original text.

The first deviation from the Isidorian model occurs immediately after the description of the dragon soaring into and disturbing the air: 'and also the see swelleth ageins his venyme'.[22] The picture painted is an upheaval of air and water through the presence of the dragon, and in the context of the sea's reaction to the dragon we have a first mention of its poison ('venyme'). The dragon's main way of killing is still by crushing its opponent, yet Trevisa modifies Isidore's categorical statement that 'it does not harm with poison' (p. 255) to 'And hath nought so moche venyme as othere serpentz' (p. 1184). So Trevisa's dragon does carry poison, though to a somewhat lesser extent than other snakes. Although Trevisa's modification does not change the way the dragon kills the elephant, it sets the stage for additional information from other sources.

Thus, Trevisa refers to Solinus as the authority for the fact that the dragon 'hath venyme oonliche (only) in his tonge and in his galle' (p. 1185). The Ethiopians therefore remove these two pieces and use the rest of its body for food and medicinal purposes. This detail is of special interest for students of literature since it explains why Tristan, after having killed the dragon and cut out its tongue to prove his deed to the king, swoons immediately after sticking the trophy into his 'hose' (i.e. leggings).[23] Had he read his Solinus or Bartholomaeus Anglicus, or at least the translation by Trevisa, he would have known better and avoided any direct contact with the tongue. Bevis of Hampton, another dragon-slayer, seems better informed (or simply luckier) since he cuts out the tongue but then sticks it onto his spear to carry.[24]

Trevisa further modifies 'does not harm with poison' in the last paragraph of his chapter on the dragon by quoting Aristotle's claim that 'dragons bytynge that eteth venemouse bestes is perilous' (p. 1186), implying a possible explanation for the variations in 'poisonousness', which would depend largely on the individual dragon's diet. This changes his earlier modification of Isidore's text from 'It has its strength not in its teeth but in its tail, and it causes injury more by its lashing tail than with its jaws' (p. 255) to the more balanced 'And hath strengthe nought oonly in teeth but also in tayl' (p. 1184). Trevisa's description is not only a better fit for the nameless *Beowulf* dragon that causes the hero's demise through its poisoned bite, but also for the other 'prince of dragons', the Old Norse Fafnir.[25] This worm does not breathe fire, but 'Hann fnýsti eitri alla leið fyrir sik fram', which Jesse L. Byock translates

as: 'He (the dragon) blew poison (*eitr*) over all the path before him.'[26] Fafnir's 'poisonous breath' had always puzzled me – until I read Trevisa's explanation for the dragon's fiery breath:

> Also Plinius seith that for might of the venyme his tonge is alwey arrered, and somtyme he setteth the ayer afuyre by hete of his venyme so that it semeth that he bloweth and casteth fuyre out of his mouth. (p. 1185)[27]

Trevisa's explanation (attributed to Pliny) reads a bit like the faux scientific theories discussed with great seriousness in the chapter 'Fiery breath' in Dickinson's twentieth-century 'dragon encyclopaedia'.[28] However, it is very unlikely that Trevisa or any of the other medieval encyclopaedists had the intention of pulling their reader's leg. The hypothesis of the poison in the dragon's tongue setting the air on fire seems to me rather in harmony with the chapter's overall endeavour of providing explanations or motivations for the phenomena described. Thus, to give another example of this tendency, Trevisa is not content to simply describe the dragon's attack on the elephant, as Isidore does, but he additionally gives his readers a 'natural' explanation for this aggressive behaviour: 'The cause why the dragon desireth his [i.e. the elephant's] blood is coldnesse of the elephantes blood by the which the dragoun desireth to kele [i.e. to cool] himself' (p. 1185). This in turn prepares the ground for yet another aspect of the dragon's strange behaviour, namely its habit of opening and turning its mouth against the wind in order to quench its burning thirst, and 'therfore whanne he seeth schippes sayle in the see in grete wynde he fleeth ageins the sayle to take there colde wynde' (p. 1185), which causes the sailors to immediately strike the sails in order to avoid a collision with the dragon.

The overall impression we get from Trevisa's chapter is that it provides a clear categorization of the dragon as a real though sometimes exotic and strange animal, and is therefore in agreement with Isidore. And although Trevisa's text is considerably longer than Isidore's and comprises much new information, he succeeds in keeping it from degenerating into an incoherent jumble of items. The fact that it retains its coherence in spite of its length is mainly due to Trevisa's endeavours to relate the different elements to each other. This way he creates an internal textual cohesion that anchors the dragon in the scientific discourse of the Middle Ages, which is all the more important since the scholarly tradition stands in fierce competition with the religious discourse – which will be the theme of the next chapter.

THE DRAGON AND MEDIEVAL RELIGION

THE BIBLICAL TRADITION

THE DRAGON IS, next to the lamb, arguably one of the most prominent creatures mentioned in the Bible. While the lamb symbolizes Christ, the dragon stands for Satan. This is made explicit in Revelation (12:7–9) where the *King James Version* gives the following account:[1]

> (7) And there was war in heaven: Michael and his angels fought against the dragon [see illustration 5]; and the dragon fought and his angels, (8) And prevailed not; neither was their place found any more in heaven. (9) And the great dragon was cast out, that old serpent, called the Devil, and Satan, which deceiveth the whole world: he was cast out into the earth, and his angels were cast out with him.[2]

For our purpose the most important information is located in verse 9, where the author equates the 'great dragon' with the 'old serpent', which is usually interpreted as a reference to the snake (*serpens*) mentioned in connection with the Fall (Genesis 3).[3] Both the 'great dragon' (*draco ille magnus*) and the 'old serpent' (*serpens antiquus*) are then identified as incarnations of Satan – a connection that has often led to

Illustration 5: *Saint Michael fighting the devil-dragon*. *Drawing by* Anke Eissmann *based on* Martin Schongauer's Saint Michael fighting the dragon (1480–90).

a conflation of the two creatures.[4] The association of the dragon with the Devil is further supported by the Old Testament reports of the antagonism between God himself or his servants and monstrous creatures – which in turn contain echoes of the older mythologies of the Near East. This is the background to the story given in the Book of Daniel 14:22–7 (*Vulgate*), which reports how the prophet Daniel makes cakes out of pitch, fat and hair in order to feed them to a dragon that is revered as a living god by the Babylonians. The dragon bursts and is destroyed, much to the displeasure of its followers. The enmity between the dragon and God himself is mentioned in Psalm 73:13–14 (*Vulgate*) and Isaiah 27:1. The Psalm passage in the *Vulgate* version reads as follows: '(13) tu dissipasti in fortitudine tua mare contrivisti capita *draconum* in aquis (14) tu confregisti capita *Leviathan* dedisti eum in escam populo Aethiopum.' This is rendered in the *King James Version* as Psalm 74:13: '(13) Thou didst divide the sea by thy strength: thou brakest the heads of the *dragons* in the waters. (14) Thou brakest the heads of *leviathan* in pieces, and gavest him to be meat to the people inhabiting the wilderness.' The point of interest here is the parallel construction with *capita draconum* ('heads of dragons') and *capita Leviathan* ('heads of Leviathan'), which suggests, if not an equation, then at the least a close proximity of the 'draco' with the Leviathan, whom we have already met in Job 41. Isaiah 27:1 corroborates this in both the *Vulgate* and the *King James Version* by referring to the Leviathan as *serpens* and 'serpent', respectively.[5]

As a result, we have a deep-rooted and stable association of the Devil and his minions with the semantic cluster comprised of the elements 'snake/Leviathan/dragon'.[6]

THE ALLEGORICAL TRADITION

Even though the dragon is a creature whose existence is unambiguously attested by the biblical texts, it has not been awarded a separate entry in the original *Physiologus*.[8] This omission was remedied in the bestiary tradition, which adopted the chapter from Isidore's *Etymologiae* as its starting point, augmented it with additional information from different sources and, as *The Book of Beasts* proves, also added an allegorical interpretation:

> The Devil, who is the most enormous of all reptiles, is like this dragon. He is often borne into the air from his den, and the air round him blazes, for the Devil in raising himself from the lower regions translates himself into an angel of light and misleads the foolish with false hopes of glory and worldly bliss. He is said to have a crest or crown because he is the King of Pride, and his strength is not in his teeth but in his tail because he beguiles those whom he draws to him by deceit, their strength being destroyed. He lies hidden round the paths on which they saunter, because their way to heaven is encumbered by the knots of their sins, and he strangles them to death. For if anybody is ensnared by the toils of crime he dies, and no doubt he goes to Hell.[10]

Unlike animals such as the lion,[11] the dragon is predominantly interpreted *in malam partem*[12] – that is, it is either associated with the Devil himself or the demons of hell – and it is in this function that it makes its appearance in the saints' lives.

SAINTS

Modern readers are likely to know at least two of the dragon-slaying saints, namely Saint Michael the Archangel and Saint George, the latter popularly associated with England. Both differ from the other dragon-slaying saints by their use of brute force rather than prayer to subdue the dragon. The credentials of Saint Michael the Archangel go back to the Old Testament (Daniel 10:13–21 and 12:1) and we have met him already as the leader of the heavenly forces in the War in Heaven in Revelation 12:7–9. Michael is thus a martial saint not bound to any particular place or time, which made him popular with soldiers of different nations and times. Most importantly, Saint Michael is one of the saints who fights the Devil himself, and not simply one of Satan's minions or a creature that represents evil allegorically or symbolically.[13] This is often forgotten by secular modern audiences, who tend to interpret the depiction of the angel battling with a dragon or dragon-like monster solely as an allegorical representation of the struggle between Good and Evil. Medievalists and the traditionally minded Christians may deplore this loss of the primary level of meaning, yet it has proved a blessing in disguise since this way the motif survived down through the ages and its universal spiritual applicability has made up for the fact that the original theological reality is no longer perceived. Thus, many of the chapels or churches built on a hill and dedicated to Saint Michael have been interpreted as foundations commemorating and proclaiming Christianity's victory over paganism in the area – often with the new Christian edifice built on the site formerly occupied by a pagan sanctuary.[14] Dominic

Alexander, for example, argues that the appearance and the defeat of dragons 'in the fourth and fifth centuries are . . . likely to represent victory over paganism'.[15] The association of the dragon with paganism may have been especially prominent in the early stages of Christian expansion, but it did not stop later on and a narrative detail from the later legend of Saint George testifies to the motif's enduring power.

Saint George was originally a martyr saint without any connection to dragons and it was only around the tenth century that the 'fight against the monster' motif in the form of his struggle with the dragon attached itself to his story.[16] The standard version of the legend relevant for most of the later Middle Ages and beyond is found in Jacobus de Voragine's *Legenda aurea* (AD *c.*1260). William Caxton, in his translation of the text (1483), gives the following account of the encounter between Saint George and the dragon:

> S. George was a knight and born in Cappadocia. On a time he came in to the province of Libya, to a city which is said Silene. And by this city was a stagne or a pond like a sea, wherein was a dragon which envenomed all the country. And on a time the people were assembled for to slay him, and when they saw him they fled. And when he came nigh the city he venomed the people with his breath, and therefore the people of the city gave to him every day two sheep for to feed him, because he should do no harm to the people, and when the sheep failed there was taken a man and a sheep. Then was an ordinance made in the town that there should be taken the children and young people of them of the town by lot, and every each one as it fell, were he gentle or poor,

should be delivered when the lot fell on him or her. So it happed that many of them of the town were then delivered, insomuch that the lot fell upon the king's daughter . . . Then did the king do array his daughter like as she should be wedded, and embraced her, kissed her and gave her his benediction, and after, led her to the place where the dragon was.

When she was there S. George passed by, and when he saw the lady he demanded the lady what she made there and she said: Go ye your way fair young man, that ye perish not also. Then said he: Tell to me what have ye and why weep ye, and doubt ye of nothing. When she saw that he would know, she said to him how she was delivered to the dragon. Then said S. George: Fair daughter, doubt ye no thing hereof for I shall help thee in the name of Jesu Christ. She said: For God's sake, good knight, go your way, and abide not with me, for ye may not deliver me. Thus as they spake together the dragon appeared and came running to them, and S. George was upon his horse, and drew out his sword and garnished him with the sign of the cross, and rode hardily against the dragon which came towards him, and smote him with his spear and hurt him sore and threw him to the ground [see illustration 6]. And after said to the maid: Deliver to me your girdle, and bind it about the neck of the dragon and be not afeard. When she had done so the dragon followed her as it had been a meek beast and debonair. Then she led him into the city, and the people fled by mountains and valleys, and said: Alas! alas! we shall be all dead. Then S. George said to them: Ne doubt ye no thing, without more, believe ye in God, Jesu Christ, and do ye to be baptized and I shall slay the dragon. Then the king was

baptized and all his people, and S. George slew the dragon and smote off his head, and commanded that he should be thrown in the fields, and they took four carts with oxen that drew him out of the city.

Then were there well fifteen thousand men baptized, without women and children, and the king did do make a church there of our Lady and of S. George, in the which yet sourdeth a fountain of living water, which healeth sick people that drink thereof. After this the king offered to

Illustration 6: *Saint George fighting the dragon. Drawing by Anke Eissmann based on Vittore Carpaccio's* (1465–1526) St George and the Dragon (1502).

> S. George as much money as there might be numbered, but he refused all and commanded that it should be given to poor people for God's sake; and enjoined the king four things, that is, that he should have charge of the churches, and that he should honour the priests and hear their service diligently, and that he should have pity on the poor people, and after, kissed the king and departed.[17]

The legend in Jacobus's version clearly features a variant of the 'rescue of the sacrificial virgin' motif known from the myths of antiquity, such as Perseus and Andromeda or Heracles and Hesione.[18] There are, however, some details in the narrative that deserve our attention. First, Saint George signs himself with the cross before attacking the dragon, but it is basically by brute force that he subdues the beast. He is thus akin to Saint Michael, the other dragon-slaying warrior saint, and stands in contrast to those who, like Saint Margaret of Antioch or Saint Martha, rely solely on the power of their prayers. Secondly, he does not kill the dragon right away, but at first merely wounds and subdues it with the help of a virgin's girdle. The narrative so far shows close parallels to other tales that feature a saint or hero subduing a monster: tales that are often interpreted as relating, in a figurative way, how elementary forces of nature and chaos threatening the human settlements have been averted or hemmed in.[19] These can be floods, earthquakes, mudslides, etc. or less tangible and therefore all the more disquieting dangers such as illnesses and diseases. Thus, the fact that the dragon is said to live in 'stagne or a pond like a sea' links it to all those numerous aquatic monsters that are often interpreted as representing the dangers

inherent in this element. Furthermore, the text explicitly mentions the noxious exhalation of the dragon as the cause of the people's suffering: 'he [the dragon] venomed the people with his breath'. The theme of disease found in the opening part of the narrative is then taken up and happily concluded by the reference to the 'healing well' that springs up at the newly founded church, 'which healeth sick people that drink thereof'. Looked at in isolation, these elements would suggest an interpretation of the legend as an aetiological tale providing the explanation for how the community of Silen was threatened by the miasmic vapours arising from the nearby swamps or stagnant ponds, which would be ideal breeding grounds for malaria or other diseases – and which would be defeated by the draining of the area. Such an interpretation could argue that the tale translated these abstract and rather unspectacular technical events into the more concrete, visual and appealing language of the folktale, presenting the intangible disease as the dragon's venomous breath and the draining of the swamp as the subduing of the beast by a hero.

So far, so good. However, the tale does not end with the marriage of the hero to the rescued princess, nor is the subdued dragon sent off into the wilderness never to trouble them again – as in the cases of the dragons in the legends of Saint Marcellus of Paris, Saint Pope Sylvester of Rome and Saint Samson of Dol. Our saint in question at first leads the tamed dragon into the town and basically blackmails its inhabitants into converting to Christianity and receiving baptism. Only then does he kill it by chopping off its head. The demise of the dragon thus goes hand in hand with, and is causally linked to, the demise of the pagan religion in the city of Silen, and the monster is obviously meant as a symbolic representation of (defeated) paganism. This is an important point since the setting of the entire adventure as given in the *Golden Legend* could, as we have seen, invite alternative readings. The author of the legend must have tried to adapt and fit the folktale of the dragon-slayer, which had not been an original part of the life of the martyr-saint, to its new hagiographical setting. He does so by overwriting the older narrative, yet without being able to obliterate it completely, thus creating a palimpsest where parts of the original version are still visible.

The Christian recension of the tale of the dragon-slayer, as given in the story of Saint George in the *Legenda Aurea*, is probably the most popular version of the narrative in both the Middle Ages and the early modern era, and its structural narrative elements have survived in adapted form in modern literature and films.[20] It has furthermore provided, directly or indirectly, the inspiration for the innumerable depictions of Saint George battling the dragon in stained-glass windows, manuscript illustrations, altarpieces, paintings, sculptures, reliefs, posters, advertisements, etc. Its importance for the development of the dragon motif is also due to its central position in the tradition. On the one hand, it takes up and continues the motif of the woman/virgin rescued from the monster. On the other, it provides the narrative blueprint and contrastive backdrop for most of the later dragon narratives. A tale such as Kenneth Grahame's 'The Reluctant Dragon' (1898) or J. R. R. Tolkien's 'Farmer Giles of Ham' (1937, published 1949) could not be properly appreciated without being conversant with the basic elements of the Saint George legend.

The interpretation of the central motif of the legend has also been adapted and applied to varying situations and used for different purposes throughout the centuries.[21] Thus the political, military or religious opponents would be identified with the dragon, while one's own side was presented as righteous and saintly (see illustration 7).

Furthermore, as Riches argues, the 'dragon and the Virgin seem to be intended to embody the polar opposites inherent in late medieval attitudes to women, the nadir and the epitome: the evil, sexual, bestial creature and the good, virginal, saintly creature'.[22] Thus the dragon episode has served different functions at different times and under different circumstances, which Riches summarizes as follows: 'It played on the deep-seated fears of uneducated people, spoke to their need to assert control over the natural world, and also served as a tool of religious propaganda and sexual politics.'[23]

The second and final group of saints to be discussed differs from Saints Michael and George in as much as they are not using physical force to defeat their monstrous opponent. Saint Samson of Dol, Saint Marcellus of Paris, Saint Martha at Aix-en-Provence and Saint Margaret of Antioch are representatives of this tradition and rely on the power of their prayers and invocations to overcome dragons. Of those, Saint Margaret of Antioch has gained greater international prominence since her Life was included in Jacobus de Voragine's *Legenda aurea*. She is believed to have lived around AD 300 and, having been brought up by a Christian woman, was baptized. The young woman attracted the attention of the Roman governor of the region, who asked for her hand in marriage. Margaret refused on religious

Illustration 7: *Saint George fighting the dragon on a recruitment poster during the* First World War. *Drawing by* Anke Eissmann *based on poster no.* 108 *issued by the* Parliamentary Recruiting Committee *in* 1915.

grounds, was arrested by the governor, tortured cruelly after her repeated refusal to marry him, and finally thrown into prison. The legend then, in the words of Caxton's translation, gives the following account of the events in the prison:

> And whilst she was in prison, she prayed our Lord that the fiend that had fought with her, he would visibly show him unto her. And then appeared a horrible dragon and assailed her, and would have devoured her, but she made the sign of the cross, and anon he vanished away. And in another place it is said that he swallowed her into his belly, she making the sign of the cross. And the belly brake asunder, and so she issued out all whole and sound.
>
> This swallowing and breaking of the belly of the dragon is said that it is [*sic*] apocryphal.[24]

Caxton gives not only the two different versions but also the qualifying comment on the 'swallowed by the dragon' episode – which had become the iconographically productive version with numerous manuscript illustrations depicting the dramatic scene of Margaret breaking through the belly of the dragon (see illustration 8).

This rather grotesque scene links her to the Old Testament figure of Jonah, who was swallowed by a whale and survived for three days and three nights in its belly until the 'big fish' delivered him onto the shore.[25] Jonah's sojourn in the belly of the whale has in turn been interpreted as a typological foreshadowing of Christ's Harrowing of Hell.[26] This means that Saint Margaret's being swallowed by the dragon evokes, for a Catholic audience, associations with Christ's deeds and Christ himself. She stands, like the other

Illustration 8: *Saint Margaret bursting from the dragon's belly. Drawing by* Anke Eissmann *based on an illustration in a fifteenth-century* Book *of* Hours (*Belgium*, c.1440; *New York*, Morgan *Library*, MS M.19, *fol.* 157*v*).

non-martial dragon-defeating saints, for the power of the faith against all kind of dangers. In her case, the dragon is clearly identified as an incarnation of satanic forces that are overcome by her patient *passio* (i.e. suffering) in imitation of Christ's passion. Hers is also a much more personal struggle than that of, for example, Saint Marcellus or Saint Sylvester, whose taming of their respective dragons presents them as representatives of Christianity performing services to their respective communities, rather than grappling with the Devil for the salvation of their virginity and their personal souls.[27]

To conclude on a different and more mundane note: the key scene of Saint Margaret bursting forth from the dragon's belly most likely motivated her inclusion among the Fourteen Holy Helpers, where she is the saint responsible for assisting in childbirth.

RELIGIOUS ART

The great majority of dragons found in the pictorial arts are closely linked to the textual traditions outlined. Their function remains thus basically the same as in the texts. What differs is, of course, the degree to which the dragon's features and looks have to be rendered explicit. Thus, the Anglo-Saxon illustrators who came first across the originally metaphorical term 'Hellmouth' visualized it not simply as an entrance but as a monstrous and real 'mouth' (see illustration 9) – and thus established the popular medieval tradition of depicting the entrance to hell as the jaws of an often dragon-like creature.

Many of the texts mentioning dragons remain tantalizingly vague and leave it up to the reader's imagination to

Illustration 9: *Jaws of hell. Drawing by* Anke Eissmann *based on a stained-glass window in* Bourges Cathedral (*twelfth century*).

flesh out the meagre information. The painter or sculptor, by contrast, has to visualize the dragon in all its details in order to depict it. They may get some inspiration from earlier artists but are not bound to their interpretations. Depictions of dragon-like monsters in scenes popular across the centuries, such as the rescue of Andromeda by Perseus,[28] Jonah's sojourn in the belly of the 'big fish' or Saint George's fight with the dragon, would provide the subject for several extensive studies.[29]

I want to limit my discussion to two examples from religious art in the widest sense of the word. They were chosen because they illustrate some of the complexities involved in visualizing dragons. The first example is the depiction of Mary as the 'Woman of the Apocalypse'. Chapter 12 of the Book of Revelation in the *King James Version* gives the following account:[30]

> (1) And there appeared a great wonder in heaven; a woman clothed with the sun, and the moon under her feet, and upon her head a crown of twelve stars ... (3) And there appeared another wonder in heaven; and behold a great red dragon, having seven heads and ten horns, and seven crowns upon his heads. (4) And his tail drew the third part of the stars of heaven, and did cast them to the earth: and the dragon stood before the woman which was ready to be delivered, for to devour her child as soon as it was born. (KJV, Revelation 12:1, 3–4) (see illustration 10)

This vision is usually interpreted as referring to the Virgin Mary giving birth to Christ, who is threatened by the Devil. The dragon is later identified explicitly as 'ille magnus *serpens*

Illustration 10: *The Woman of the Apocalypse. Drawing by* Anke Eissmann *based on a mid-thirteenth-century manuscript illustration* (*Morgan Apocalypse*, MS M.524, *fol.* 8*v*).

antiquus qui vocatur Diabolus et Satanas' (Revelation 12:9), that is, 'that old serpent, called the Devil, and Satan' and thus linked to the serpens/snake responsible for the Fall of Mankind in Paradise. This has led artists to connect the description of the figure of the Woman of the Apocalypse in the last book of the Bible with the reference to the enmity between Eve and her descendants and the snake in the first book of the Bible. God addresses the snake after the Fall: 'And I will put enmity between thee and the woman, and between thy seed and her seed; it shall bruise thy head, and thou shalt bruise his heel' (Genesis 3:15).[31] The fusion of these two elements has given us the 'Mondsichelmadonna',

that is, the Virgin Mary who stands on a crescent moon and crushes the snake-dragon beneath her foot. A depiction of this 'Mondsichelmadonna' can be found, for example, in Geertgen tot Sint Jans's *The Glorification of the Virgin* (*c.*1480) (see illustration 11).[32] The artist has combined the different elements, translated their theological interpretation into a visually explicit form, and thus contributed to the continued identification of the Devil with the snake in Paradise.

Our second example takes us to Lucerne, an ancient Swiss town situated on the shores of Lake Lucerne and overshadowed by Mount Pilatus. Lucerne has a long tradition of dragon sightings and is rich in folklore accounts featuring these and other monsters.[33] The dragons relevant for this chapter are, however, to be found neither in the depths of the lake nor on the heights of Mount Pilatus but on the back of a fifteenth-century chasuble (see illustration 12).

The central back section of this vestment consists of two pieces of light blue silk, each showing a Chinese dragon framed by little white clouds. The existence of Chinese silks north of the Alps is known from other instances,[35] but in the case of the Lucerne chasuble the presence of two dragons must have raised some questions. The original Lucerne audience, in spite of the considerable culture gap between the Chinese and the European dragon traditions, must have easily identified the two creatures as members of the *draco* family. Dragons were familiar from local folklore, from chronicle accounts, from literary narratives and, of course, also as part of the Christian religious imaginary. It was thus not the two dragons per se that required an explanation, but the way and the place they were presented. Had it been a depiction of Saint George fighting or of Saint

Illustration 11: *'Mondsichelmadonna'. Drawing by Anke Eissmann based on Geertgen tot Sint Jans's* (AD *c.*1460–*c.*1490) The Glorification of the Virgin (*c.*1480).

Illustration 12: *Chasuble with Chinese silks depicting dragons. Lucerne* (Switzerland) *c.*1400.[36] *Drawing by* Anke Eissmann.

Sylvester taming their respective dragons, the presence of the beasts would have been self-explanatory. This way, however, we have two representatives of evil frolicking on a piece of clothing used in the central Christian ritual of the mass without even the shadow of a saint discernible. Whatever the original motivation for the inclusion of the pieces of Chinese silk in the chasuble, it soon gave rise to an aetiological tale reported for the first time by Renward Cysat (1545–1614). He recorded it in 1580 but adds that it had been handed down for at least four generations, so that Reinle dates the events to *c.*1410.[37] The narrative claims that the chasuble had been sponsored by a grateful cooper in order to express his thanks for his miraculous rescue from a very uncomfortable situation indeed.[38] This cooper climbs Mount Pilatus in autumn in search of willow trees suitable for cask-making. He falls into a deep crevice and ends up between two dragons that have chosen this spot as their winter quarters. Luckily, they ignore the hapless cooper, who survives the winter months by praying to the Virgin for deliverance and by imitating the dragons, who keep themselves nourished by licking the liquid oozing from the rock. With the coming of spring, first one and then the other dragon spreads its wings and flies off – the second with the cooper dangling from its tail, who is thus able to finally leave the crevice and return home. Mindful of his vows to the Virgin, he sponsors a chasuble with embroidery telling the tale of his miraculous rescue.

Assuming that the extant fifteenth-century chasuble is the piece in question, we cannot but notice the difference between what, according to Cysat's tale, was depicted on the chasuble, namely the story of the cooper's predicament and his miraculous rescue, and what we actually have, namely two Chinese dragons and no cooper at all.[39] Whether this is yet another instance of a medieval dissociation between image and text or whether there are other explanations cannot be discussed here.[40]

For our purpose, the main importance of the Lucerne chasuble and the concomitant aetiological tale lies in their ability to illustrate the ways in which exotic, foreign and potentially irritating elements are incorporated and functionally integrated into an existing framework. We know that the Chinese dragon is usually positively connoted, in contrast to its counterparts in the Western (Judeo-Christian) tradition.[41] As a consequence, the Chinese dragon occurs as a stand-alone motif on official and ceremonial vestments. A similar use in a medieval Christian context would be highly problematic and would have to be hedged against misunderstandings. Lucerne seems to offer an ideal environment for such an operation since dragons were not only prominently represented in folklore and chronicle accounts, but were also inscribed in the very landscape through the connection of places and mountains with the numerous sightings and realia such as the 'Pilatusdrachen' ('Mount Pilatus dragon') and the famous 'Luzerner Drachenstein' ('Dragonstone of Lucerne').[42] We have thus a secular, non-religious framework where dragons were accepted as part of the local fauna and tradition. These circumstances made it possible that, in this particular case, the religious dragon narrative could be replaced by an alternative one. As a consequence, we have the rather unique case (at least in an explicitly Christian context) of pictorially unhedged dragons without the usual demonic connotations.

The two case studies discussed show that dragons are able to adapt to new (cultural) environments and even survive transfers across time and culture(s). The compiler of the legend of Saint George, for example, faced the challenge of how to adapt a non-biblical dragon to the new Christian framework, and the tale illustrates how the beast, which originally represented the non-spiritual dangers of untamed nature, was re-interpreted in a religious-moral sense.[43] The two Chinese dragons on the chasuble, by contrast, are not interpreted as representations of evil, which would have incorporated them into the conventional Christian framework. Instead, the aetiological tale that has attached itself to the enigmatic chasuble links them to the dragons of Lucerne folklore and grounds them in a secular-popular framework. It is this world of popular tales and folklore that we are going to explore in the next chapter.

THE MEDIEVAL DRAGON AND FOLKLORE

THE DRAGON OF folklore has been the (implicit) subject of the two publications by Jacqueline Simpson and is usually given at least a chapter of its own in almost all books on dragons – most recently in Martin Arnold's excellent monograph *The Dragon. Fear and Power.*[1] Yet while these studies provide us with a plethora of references to and information about popular stories and folktales featuring dragons, the tales supplied are not based on medieval texts directly since the narratives are available only in their post-medieval versions. We do have dragons in medieval texts that carry the whiff of the folk-tale, such as the two dragons fighting with each other in the story of Vortigern and Merlin, yet we do not have the folktale proper.[2] And neither Walter Map (AD 1140–1210), who talks about vampires, the Wild Hunt and numerous other interesting phenomena, nor Gerald of Wales (AD 1146–1223), another enthusiastic collector of medieval folklore *avant la lettre*, so much as mentions the dragon. This dearth of genuinely medieval evidence constitutes a general problem of folklore studies and is not limited to dragons. Take, for example, the 'Man in the Moon', who occurs in Shakespeare's *A Midsummer Night's Dream* and who is the subject of several popular nursery rhymes. It is by mere luck that we have some scattered surviving medieval references that allow us to reconstruct a possible narrative for the Man in the Moon.[3] Unfortunately, we don't have even such piece-meal and chance references for the dragon of folklore. This is due also to the fact that the dragon of folklore shares much common ground with the worms found in the texts[4] of canonical literature, religion and (medieval) science. Dragons in contexts such as the lost medieval folktale, medieval pageants and processions[5] were seen as part of a wider framework and, unlike the Man in the Moon, were not perceived as a feature typical of or limited to folklore.[6] This, of course, changes in post-medieval times when dragons were not only expelled from the realm of natural science, but also from the more realistic literary genres of the novel and the drama. They survived in the religious imagery of Catholic countries, in the popular adaptations of medieval narratives (such as the broadsheet ballads) and, most importantly, also in folktales. It would take almost another two centuries until the first collectors of folk- and fairy tales published the results of their endeavours in book-form, thus allowing the folklore dragon to resurface at long last from orality into print. However, the late entry of the folklore dragon into the world of print meant that it encountered an environment that had changed considerably because its siblings had disappeared from non-religious literature and science. As a consequence, it would no longer be seen as part of a more wide-ranging tradition but interpreted as a feature typical of the folk- and fairy tale. This is arguably one reason why Andrew Lang included a shortened and simplified version of the *Völsunga Saga* as 'The Story of Sigurd' in his *The Red Fairy Book* (1890). The prominent position of the dragon Fafnir qualified the narrative at the heart of the Old Norse epic as a folktale, whose ancient core could be recovered by retelling the story in the language of the folktale. Lang accordingly opens 'The Story of Sigurd' with 'ONCE upon a time there was a King in the North'.[7] The result is, however, not entirely satisfactory, mostly because Lang did not sufficiently reduce the complexity of the epic narrative[8] and unintentionally proves that the translation from one genre into another is not that easy. Indeed, the relationships between the folktale and its related genres, such as the fairy tale and the enigmatic nursery rhymes on the one hand, and the more literary medieval genres such as the lay,[9] the epic or the (courtly) romance, on the other, are complex. The idea of the 'the Cauldron of Story, (that) has always been boiling, and to [... which] have continually been added new bits, dainty and undainty' offers an attractive solution to describe the nature of the often elusive and puzzling connections between the different genres and literary motifs.[10] The concept of the 'Cauldron of Story' proposes that authors, poets, narrators, storytellers, etc. of all ages have accessed an unstructured and indiscriminating common source of motifs, characters, plot elements, etc. It does not presuppose a temporal or (implicitly) hierarchical progression from archaic and primitive forms to more sophisticated and complex texts but sees the different motifs and elements as freely available for a re-working and re-combination in the different literary genres on all levels and throughout the centuries.

The dragon, then, is one of those elements that has been floating around in the Cauldron of Story since time

immemorial, and it does not come as a surprise that it ended up in a great number of soups. The dragon has featured prominently in the cosmic creation myths of numerous cultures, found a place in the foundation myths of various nations, been chosen to represent the Devil in Christianity, become the ultimate adversary for the epic hero or saint, and also constitutes one of the major challenges for the folktale hero.

I have chosen the tale of the Mordiford Dragon to explore the characteristics of the 'medieval' dragon in the folktale. The story has a wide circulation and can be found, for example, in Simpson's *British Dragons* (1980), Shuker's *Dragons* (1995), and is one of the three British dragon folktales discussed by Martin Arnold in his recent *The Dragon* (2018). The presentation of the story is, however, not always satisfactory and illustrates some of the difficulties that arise when we try to establish an authoritative version of an allegedly orally transmitted folktale. Shuker, for example, is silent about his sources and gives his readers merely a 'chivalric' version, identifying the hero as a member of 'Mordiford's most illustrious family, the Garstons', who kills the dragon in a fair fight.[11] I shall base my discussion on the version(s) first published and discussed by James Dacres Devlin in 1848 under the title *The Mordiford Dragon*.[12] His study gives us not only variant versions of the tale but also takes into account written and oral sources. Furthermore, he provides what we could call a critical discussion of sources and possible (historical and scientific) explanations for the story's origin. Last, and this may be more the brainchild of Devlin's poetic impulse than the product of his scholarly endeavours, he entertains his readers with his own renderings of the narrative's three versions in verse. Devlin's publication is thus an excellent example of how the concept of the Cauldron of Story works – both for scholarly analysis and for the creation of new literary texts.

The first part of the tale is prefaced by Devlin's assurance of having (probably) first-hand knowledge of the tale in an oral form.[13] He not only links his narrative firmly to the oral tradition but also pushes it back in time as far as possible by having his unnamed informant telling him that

> while living at Bishop Hampton, the adjoining village, on the Hereford side, to Mordiford, he often heard an old man of the name of Wigley, then nearly a centenarian in years, discourse of the far-famed Dragon of the *locale* of his birth; and this, in its early part, was the relation he gave, though perhaps not altogether couched in his own language. (pp. 4–5)

What follows (pp. 6–13) is the first part of the tale, that is, relating how 'Long, long ago' (p. 6) a young girl called Maud finds a small green dragon while gathering blackberries. The rather detailed description of the young dragon (p. 6) tells the informed reader that it must be a young wyvern (see illustration 13):[14]

> [For] now more fully appeared one of the most beautiful little creatures imaginable, being scarcely the size of a cucumber, and in form of its body very much like this oblong growing root. It sprung forth before her with a sort of flying hop ... Its whole frame was the colour of the greenest grass; it had a slender pointed tail . . . Wings,

> too, it had, even as a pretty bird; and legs, also, like a bird, or like herself, though these legs were very short. But the greater fascination was about its head, it was so exquisitely sloping from the skull down to the extreme of its mouth. And the eyes! – the eyes appeared as brilliant as the very stars themselves, and always in dazzling movement. (p. 6)

The girl takes it back home to her parents' house and raises it in secret on a diet of milk until it has grown so much that it has to feed on more substantial fare. The wyvern then starts to attack hens, ducks and geese, and later sheep and cows, and finally does not even refrain from killing humans. Only Maud remains safe and the bond of affection between the now full-sized wyvern and the girl is as strong as ever.[15]

So far, so good. The first part has no variant and seems to be based solely on the authority of the tale told by Mr Wigley. It feels familiar, maybe because it shares elements with the Beauty and the Beast type of folktale, even though it does not match closely any of the (sub-) categories of the Aarne-Thomson-Uther classification system. Furthermore, we have the traditional pairing of the dragon with the virgin (girl), yet in a somewhat unexpected configuration that anticipates the ironic-parodistic subversions by later fantasy writers.

The textual complications seem to arise only with the second part of the story, namely the 'killing of the dragon' narrative proper. The starting point in all three versions discussed by Devlin is the same, that is, that the inhabitants of Mordiford and the surrounding landscape want to put an end to the monster's atrocities. Yet the three tales differ as

Illustration 13: A *young wyvern*. Drawing by Anke Eissmann.

to how and by whose hand the dragon meets its demise. I follow in my discussion the sequence of Devlin's poetic recreations.

The first version (pp. 44–8) introduces an unnamed convict who is given the choice between execution and fighting the serpent.[16] He heroically chooses the latter, is given a sword and sent on his way. He seeks out the dragon in its lair, attacks it bravely and finally succeeds in killing it. He cuts out the monster's tongue (p. 46) and brings it back as proof of the dragon's demise.[17] The people rejoice in his victory and they agree to commemorate the deed by means of a painting in the church.

Devlin is obviously very taken by this version and comments:

> This is one of my own picking up during a ramble in the locality concerned . . . It is, too, as I consider, the most feasible, and, therefore, engaging version, having nothing of either the barrel absurdity about it, as related in the second, nor the mere commonplace of the third. . . (p. 19)

Interestingly, it is by and large the version that appears, with a few modifications, in Shuker (pp. 48–51). Furthermore, this version of the story shows close parallels to a tale found in Petermann Etterlin's *Kronica von der loblichen Eydtgnoschaft* (1507), where a certain Winckelried is given the chance to atone for manslaughter by confronting the dragon that was terrorizing the inhabitants of Wil (Unterwalden).[18] Like the nameless convict of Devlin's first version, Winckelried manages to defeat the dragon in a fair fight, yet dies from the effects of the dragon's poisonous blood that had run down his sword and come into contact with his bare skin. This motif of the poisoned victor is familiar from *Beowulf* and, to some extent, also Tristan, and recurs, much later, in J. R. R. Tolkien's *The Children of Húrin* – and in Devlin's second version.[19]

Devlin's second poetic re-telling of the story (pp. 48–51) again introduces the man who is going to kill the monster as 'criminally disgrace'd' (p. 49). Yet this time he does not seek a direct confrontation with the dragon but, being 'more cunning than he was courageous' (p. 49), hides in a barrel that is placed in the spot where the dragon is wont to drink. Thus concealed, he watches the place through a spyhole in the barrel, and when the dragon arrives, the monster begins to 'investigate' the strange object. The man gets a chance to stab the beast through the spyhole into its belly, then jumps out of the barrel and kills the dragon after a long battle. 'And yet how sad! expiring as it lay, / Writhing its wings and tail in dreadful caper, / It breath'd upon the man in desp'rate way, / When lifeless fell he, too, from that fell vapour!' (p. 51).

This is very close to the narrative found in the oldest extant version, first published in Samuel Ireland's *Picturesque Views on the River Wye* (1797).[20] A very similar account is also given in George Lipscombe's *Journey into South Wales, through the counties of Oxford, Warwick, Worcester, Hereford, Salop, Stafford, Buckingham, and Hertford; in the year 1799*, which was published in 1802 and which is extensively quoted by Devlin.[21] Both authors introduce their report about the dragon by means of a reference to the depiction of the serpent on one of the walls of Mordiford church.[22] Lipscombe (p. 71) writes:

> and the east end (of the church) is decorated with a painting of a large green dragon. An ornament so unusual, and so seemingly unconnected with the nature and design of a place of worship, naturally excited our curiosity; which, after some enquiries, was gratified by the following story.

The relationship between the pictorial representation of the dragon/serpent and the narrative given reminds us of the case of the 'Chinese dragons chasuble' of Lucerne, where the existence of a similarly puzzling depiction gave rise to the aetiological tale of the cooper and the two dragons. Whatever the origin[23] of the now lost picture on one of the walls of Mordiford church, it served until its destruction (*c.*1811) as a constant visual reminder of the events connected to the dragon and, for lack of a written record, functioned as the stable element in the universe of oral storytelling.[24]

It is a testimony to the folk origin of the tale that we have varying versions given at different times by different narrators. If we believe Lipscombe's statement that this 'story is told with great seriousness, and confidently believed, in all its particulars, by hundreds, and perhaps by thousands of persons, whose fathers and grandfathers have handed it down to them' (p. 72), then we cannot but expect some variation in a matter that has been and, as Devlin's report proves, is still told and re-told among the population of Mordiford at large. And, indeed, one of the variants collected from oral sources has the additional detail of the spiked barrel, the poor man's version of the spiked armour used by John Lambton when battling the Lambton Worm in the eponymous tale. Devlin describes the spiking of the barrel as follows:

> [The] man had so prepared the barrel for a resolute defence, that its appearance, when placed at anchor on the Lug, was most formidable. It was bristled all over with long, sharp pointed pieces of the best manufactured steel, so that when the dragon, in its anger, began to furiously lash on the offensive object with its tail, it thus was the means of wounding itself in most frightful manner. (p. 23)

Yet in spite of these variations we can clearly discern the core elements that occur in the earliest recorded versions. Thus, both Ireland and Lipscombe include the barrel trick in its un-spiked version, and also the death of both dragon and man. However, neither of them mentions the girl Maud nor the childhood of the dragon. Furthermore, Lipscombe is very critical of the truthfulness of the dragon-slaying story: he points out its many 'ridiculous improbabilities' (p. 73) and asks, maybe rhetorically, why the killing of the dragon was 'left to the precarious issue of single combat, when the *posse commitatus* might have been easily assembled to subdue so dreadful a pest' (p. 73). He refrains, however, from altering the narrative as given by his source and thus unwittingly shows literary prudence since, as we will see in the next chapter, the confrontation between hero and monster follows the archetypal pattern of single combat, and an angry mob finishing off a dragon would constitute a grievous violation of genre conventions.[25]

The main difference to Devlin's favoured first version is that the protagonist kills the dragon with the help of a trick – which Devlin obviously finds somewhat objectionable. Thus, he not only omits completely the unsportsmanlike

spiking of the barrel in his second poetic retelling, but also minimizes the amount of the jabbing through the hole in a barrel, and has his protagonist jump out of his hiding place to finish off the dragon more heroically, face to snout. The idea of defeating the monster by means of a trick is ancient. We have mentioned before the spiked armour of John Lambton as a close analogue to the spiked barrel. Further away in time and method, but still belonging to the category of tricks, is the prophet Daniel, in the eponymous Book of Daniel 14:22–7 (*Vulgate*), who literally explodes the dragon of Bel by feeding it cakes made out of pitch, fat and hair. And even the great dragon-slayer hero of the North, Sigurd/Siegfried, does not kill Fafnir in a frontal attack but, according to the *Völsunga Saga*, digs several ditches on the track Fafnir uses, hides in one of them, and 'when the serpent crawled over the pit, Sigurd plunged the sword up under the left shoulder, so that it sank to the hilt'.[26] Furthermore, Ragnar Lothbrok uses allegedly specially prepared protective breeches (hence his nickname meaning 'hairy breeches') for his confrontation with a dragon, and even Beowulf brings along a purpose-made metal shield to even the odds in the confrontation with the fire-breathing dragon.

Devlin's third version (pp. 51–5) looks like a passage from a chronicle rather than a (folk)tale. It lacks a plot and, cutting the verbose padding of the introductory stanzas, can be summarized as follows:

> Long ago, the river Lugg was home to a monstrous creature, part fish, part beast, that had descended from an otherwise extinct pre-historic species. It grew to such a size that it started to attack even humans. When the river

> Lugg, after flooding its banks, retreated back into its bed, the villagers of Mordiford saw that the serpent-dragon, which had devoured an entire ox, had fallen asleep on the now dry land adjoining the river. They picked up their scythes, axes, pitchforks and iron-toothed rakes, and put an end to the creature.

The narrative, stripped down to the core, reads very much like an entry in a handbook of cryptozoology quoting parallels and analogues to the Loch Ness monster phenomena. As pointed out, its greatest deficiency is its lack of narrative structure. The events are not causally linked to each other and there is no element of human interest because the tragic-heroic figure of the convicted criminal is replaced by an anonymous mob.

Arnold, in his chapter 'Dragons in the Anti-establishment Folktale', discusses the Mordiford Wyvern next to the Lambton Worm, the Wawel Dragon (Krakow), the Stoor Worm (Orkney) and the Dragon of Wantley.[27] All of them, he argues, contain elements that can be interpreted as expressing criticism of the ruling classes. In the case of the Mordiford Wyvern, the monster is likely to represent both aspects of the Garstons, the leading local family: once as oppressors of the populace (dragon), and once as having a representative of their family atoning for former misdeeds (the convicted criminal). They would thus simply cancel each other out and, with the passing of time, 'as both the wyvern *and* its ill-fated slayer, the Garstons ceased to have any significance whatsoever, except, that is, as either an old memory or, more likely, a current perception of class injustice'.[28]

Whatever the possible socio-political or (local) historical meaning(s) behind the tale, Devlin's presentation of the matter in his 1848 publication may be seen primarily as an illustration of the Cauldron of Story in full bloom. As mentioned before, we can identify the individual elements of 'condemned criminal turned dragon-slayer', 'trick used to defeat the worm' and, at least in some versions, 'victorious hero killed by the defeated dragon's poison'. These are all motives well known from other narratives that attach themselves to the Mordiford Wyvern in varying combinations. On a higher, more structural level we have the linking of two larger narrative blocks. Devlin, taking the orally transmitted account of the wyvern's early years as given by the nonagenarian Mr Wigley, makes it into the first part of a more fully rounded narrative by joining it to the independently-attested and already-published tale of the dragon-slayer. Devlin seems to follow in the footsteps of people like the *Beowulf* poet, who also combined two originally independent narrative blocks to achieve a new overall structural balance.[29] In Devlin's case, however, the success is only partial since he failed to exploit the full potential inherent in such a combination. He seems to forget about Maud once he discusses the dragon-slayer episode proper, and thus leaves it to later authors to complete the fusion of the two parts into a coherent narrative. It is anthologists such as Shuker who continue along the lines indicated by Devlin/Wigley, and Shuker (p. 51) actually improves on Devlin's published version by mentioning in the last paragraph of his retelling about the distraught Maud mourning her murdered childhood friend.[30] Although in no way fully developed, it at least preserves an aspect that could be elaborated further in other retellings, focusing the story on the feelings of the young girl and her rather unusual companion.

The Mordiford dragon, whom Lipscombe (p. 71) described as depicted on the Mordiford church wall as 'a large green dragon', has been floating in the Cauldron of Story for quite some time, and it may be this particular green morsel that ended up in young Tolkien's first attempt at story writing. In a letter to W. H. Auden (dated 7 June 1955), he remembers:

> I first tried to write a story when I was about seven. It was about a dragon. I remember nothing about it except a philological fact. My mother said nothing about the dragon, but pointed out that one could not say 'a green great dragon', but had to say 'a great green dragon'. I wondered why, and still do. The fact that I remember this is possibly significant, as I do not think I ever tried to write a story again for many years, and was taken up with language.[31]

It once more appears in Tolkien's poem 'The Dragon's Visit', which opens

> The dragon lay on the cherry trees
> a-simmering and a-dreaming:
> Green was he, and the blossom white,
> and the yellow sun gleaming.[32]

However, for Tolkien the green dragon of folklore proved a dead end, and it is dragons such as Glaurung or Smaug, which were inspired by the dragons in medieval (epic) literature, that gained him world-wide fame.

THE DRAGON AND MEDIEVAL LITERATURE

THE DRAGON IN medieval literature[1] is a close relative to the dragon of the scholarly tradition and likewise related to the serpent of the folktale. It is only indirectly linked to the dragon of the religious tradition, although we have texts where the boundaries have become blurred due to cross-genre pollination. The most famous example of such an ambiguous dragon in English medieval literature is probably the one found in the Middle English romance *Bevis of Hampton*, which will be discussed in detail in the second part of this chapter. The first part will focus on the *wyrm* found in the Old English epic *Beowulf*, whom we have already encountered at the beginning of this study, and on the development of the epic dragon in later texts.

BEOWULF – AND BEYOND

Beowulf,[2] sometimes erroneously dubbed 'The Epic of England',[3] is not only one of the earliest but also the only surviving representative in English of the originally pagan Germanic epic tradition. The sole extant manuscript has survived the vicissitudes of time and even the fire at Ashburnham House in 1731, so that we have the poem,

at 3182 lines, almost in its entirety. The manuscript dates to the end of the tenth or beginning of the eleventh century, though most parts of the narrative itself are likely to go back to the seventh or even sixth century. Indeed, the events of the first part, when young Beowulf and his companions visit the Danish king Hrothgar, are embedded in a largely historical setting and we know many of the other protagonists – though not Beowulf himself – from other sources.[4] The poem is usually divided into two parts, with the first part (lines 1–1913) containing the heroic exploits of the young Geatish warrior Beowulf in Denmark, where he first fights and defeats the troll-like monster Grendel, who has haunted King Hrothgar's hall for years. He also seeks out and kills Grendel's monstrous mother in her underwater lair. The second half (lines 1914–3182) starts with a recapitulation of the events in the preceding part and then, with only a brief transitional passage (lines 2200–10a), proceeds rather hurriedly to a period more than half a century after Beowulf's visit to Hrothgar's court. The narrator informs us that Beowulf eventually succeeded his uncle Hygelac as the ruler of the Geats and that he has successfully held the throne for more than fifty years. But now his realm and his people are threatened by a fire-breathing, winged dragon that has been inadvertently awoken by a fugitive serf who stole a golden cup from the dragon's hoard.[5] Yet, before describing the depredations wrought by the irate dragon, the poet fills in his audience on the origin of the hoard (lines 2231b–70a). The poem relates how the last member of a tribe or house buries the treasure inside a newly constructed barrow before he eventually dies, too.[6] But then the dragon comes:

Hordwynne fond,
eald úhtsceaða opene standan
sé ðe byrnende biorgas séceð
nacod níðdraca· nihtes fléogeð
fýre befangen· hyne foldbúend
: : : : : : : : : : : :nan. Hé gesécean sceall
hearm on hrúsan þaér hé haéðen gold
warað wintrum fród· ne byð him wihte ðý sél.

Hoard-joy he found,
the old twilight-scather, standing open,
he who, burning, seeks barrows,
the naked malevolent dragon; he flies by night,
encircled in fire; him earth-dwellers
: : : : : : : : : : : : He has to seek
harm in the ground, where he heathen gold
guards, wise in winters; he is not a bit better for that.
(*Beowulf*, lines 2270b–7)

The description of the dragon as hunting out barrows in search of underground treasure and then jealously guarding his hoard reads very much like a characterization that could be found in a medieval encyclopaedia or bestiary. Furthermore, the information seems to be part of traditional Germanic lore about these beasts,[7] as the same elements occur in the Old English *Maxims* II[8] and form the background for Fafnir's transformation in the Old Norse *Völsunga Saga*. Unfortunately, we have no further surviving examples for this distinguishing element of a dragon mindset, yet the Anglo-Saxonist and *Beowulf* expert J. R.R. Tolkien provided an excellent character study

of this type of hoard-guarding *draco* in the figure of Smaug in *The Hobbit* (1937). The *Beowulf*-poet,[9] by contrast, takes fewer liberties with his dragon since, as a highly educated Christian author writing for a medieval Christian audience, he was treading a fine line between the 'allegorical dragon' of the Bible and the 'natural dragon' of the medieval encyclopaedic tradition. To have his dragon speak like Fafnir or Smaug, for example, would have tipped the scales too much towards the dragon's symbolic meaning(s). He may have his hero wonder whether he had unwittingly provoked the anger of God (*Beowulf*, lines 2329–31a), thus linking the dragon with the Old Testament instances of God punishing the disobedient Israelites with (very real) political and natural disasters. The description of the dragon's attacks and the devastations wrought by the irate beast support a primarily naturalistic reading and stand in contrast to the often very brief accounts of the dragons' misdeeds in the saints' lives or the folktale tradition. The poet successfully captures the fear felt by the defenceless Geats and transmits it to his audience. Hoping to strike at least a spark of terror in a modern audience, I quote it in full.

Đá se gæst ongan glédum spíwan,
beorht hofu bærnan· bryneléoma stód
eldum on andan· nó ðaér áht cwices
láð lyftfloga laéfan wolde·
wæs þæs wyrmes wíg wíde gesýne
nearofáges níð néan ond feorran·
hú se gúðsceaða Géata léode
hatode ond hýnde· hord eft gescéat
dryhtsele dyrnne aér dæges hwíle·

> hæfde landwara   líge befangen
> baéle ond bronde·   beorges getrúwode
> wíges ond wealles·   him séo wén geléah.
>
> Then the demon began   to spew flames,
> to burn bright houses;   the gleam of fire rose
> to the horror of the men;   nor there anything alive
> the hateful air-flier   wished to leave;
> the war-strength of that wyrm was   widely seen,
> the malice of the darkly cunning one   near and far,
> how the war-scather   the people of the Geats
> hated and humiliated;   back to his hoard he shot,
> the hidden lord-hall   ere the time of day;
> the inhabitants of the land had been   seized by flame,
> in blaze and in fire;   his barrow he trusted,
> his war-skill and his walls;   him this belief deceived.
> (*Beowulf*, lines 2312–23)

The dragon's fury is also explicitly linked to the theft of the cup from its hoard and though the surprised Geats must have seen it at first as the product of a malicious and capricious fate, Beowulf soon uncovers the true reason (*Beowulf*, lines 2403–5). The dragon's attacks are thus no longer simply a visitation sent by an angry God but can be causally linked to the actions of a specific person. These rather detailed and extensive descriptions of the dragon's rampage as well as the causal motivation of its actions have the effect that any allegorical or symbolic meanings are relegated to second place.

The destruction of the Geatish royal hall (*Beowulf*, lines 2324–7a) must have reminded Beowulf of Hrothgar and

the visitation of his great hall Heorot by Grendel. Yet while Beowulf had back then successfully grappled with and subdued the monster with his bare hands, he knows that a dragon is a different type of animal and that he only has a chance if he confronts it with the proper equipment. He orders a special iron shield to be made, which will protect him from the dragon's fiery breath while a normal wooden shield would burn to cinders (*Beowulf*, lines 2337–41a). This is a piece of realism skilfully woven into the otherwise archetypal encounter with the dragon, as is the narrator's comment explaining Beowulf's decision to face the dragon alone:

> Oferhogode ðá hringa fengel
> þæt hé þone wídflogan weorode gesóhte
> sídan herge· nó hé him þám sæcce ondréd
>
> Then he scorned, the rings' lord,
> that he the wide-flier would seek out with a troop,
> a large army; he did not the strife dread for himself,
> (*Beowulf*, lines 2345–7)

Here the poet-narrator is negotiating between the different levels of his narrative. On the one hand, he implies that Beowulf actually considered assembling a large army in order to deal with the dragon – which would have constituted a *novum* in medieval literature, yet which makes good sense from a realistic point of view. And this seems to be the intended effect: to anchor the dragon firmly in the world of hard facts. Suggesting to the audience that this beast can be fought with an army makes sure that it is not (primarily) perceived as, for example, an allegory of sin.

On the other hand, the passage relies on the audience's familiarity with the standards of heroic behaviour and its depiction in heroic poetry. Germanic heroes do not hedge their bets, nor do they worry overmuch about their chances of survival but are concerned rather with *lof*, 'praise, glory'.[10] The verb used to express this attitude here is *ofer-hycgan*,[11] 'to despise, to scorn', which is related to *ofer-hygd*, 'pride, arrogance', which in turn belongs to the same semantic field as the infamous *ofermod* found in the Old English poem *The Battle of Maldon*.[12] It is the same proud heroic spirit that, on the one hand, makes the leader of the Anglo-Saxon army give up his strategic advantage at Maldon and allow the invading Vikings to cross onto the mainland and, on the other, motivates Beowulf to scorn attacking the dragon with an army. Ordinary people may consider taking unfair advantage of superior numbers to kill a dragon, as did the villagers in one of the versions of the tale of the 'Dragon of Mordiford', yet for a proper epic hero it simply would not do to kill a dragon in any other way than in single combat.[13] This is why Tristan, Yvain, Lancelot, Bevis of Hampton, Guy of Warwick, Torrent of Portingale, Wigalois, Wolfdietrich and numerous other knights face their dragons alone. And as Professor Tolkien noted in his lecture on *Beowulf* (1936) about Sigurd, the slayer of Fafnir: 'the slaying of [the dragon is] the chief deed of the greatest of heroes'.[14] The same could be said about Beowulf, since the fight against the dragon is a gruelling trial that tests the aged warrior's physical and mental strength to the utmost. At about one hundred lines[15] it is much longer than, for example, the fight between Sigurd and Fafnir, and it constitutes the carefully prepared climax of the poem. I cannot quote it in

full but even a short passage will give an idea of the evocative power of the Old English alliterative long line.

gewát ðá byrnende gebogen scríðan,
tó gescipe scyndan· scyld wél gebearg
lífe ond líce laéssan hwíle
maérum þéodne þonne his myne sóhte·
ðaér hé þý fyrste forman dógore
wealdan móste swá him wyrd ne gescráf
hréð æt hilde: hond úp ábraéd
Géata dryhten· gryrefáhne slóh
incgeláfe þæt sío ecg gewác
brún on báne· bát unswíðor
þonne his ðíodcyning þearfe hæfde
bysigum gebaéded. Þá wæs beorges weard
æfter heaðuswenge on hréoum móde·
wearp wælfýre· wíde sprungon
hildeléoman.

went then burning gliding coiled,
hastening to his destiny; the shield defended well
life and body for a lesser time
the famed chieftain, then his mind desired,
where he that time for the first day
had to wield it, as Fate had not decreed for him
glory in battle: he raised up his hand,
the Geatish lord; the ghastly-hued one he struck
with his ancestoral sword, so that the edge weakened
bright on bone, bit less fiercely
than its tribe-king had need
driven in distress. Then the barrow's ward was

Illustration 14: *Beowulf fighting the dragon. Drawing by* Anke *Eissmann.*

> after the war-blow   in a fierce spirit;
> he spewed slaughter-fire;   widely spread
> battle-light.
> (*Beowulf*, lines 2569–84a)

Things do not go well for our hero and the realism noted earlier in the poem is continued also in the description of the conflict between man and beast. Beowulf may have

the strength of thirty men and an iron shield to protect himself from the dragon's fiery breath, but this is to little avail against such a huge and seemingly invulnerable opponent. Luckily, one of Beowulf's companions, whom he had left behind before approaching the entry of the barrow, takes heart and comes to his aid.[16] Together they renew the attack against the dragon and though Beowulf is wounded, they are finally able to kill the monster. It is not quite clear how and where exactly they manage to stab the dragon and the text seems to recreate the blur and confusion of the fight. All we get to know is that Wiglaf, Beowulf's nephew and the one retainer who has come to his help, is stabbing the dragon 'nioðor hwéne' (*Beowulf*, line 2699), which can be translated as 'somewhat lower down' and that Beowulf himself finishes it off by hitting the 'wyrm on middan' (*Beowulf*, line 2705), that is, 'in the middle'. This is rather vague but if we combine it with the information about the dragon from the preceding passages and complement it with what we know from other sources, textual and pictorial,[17] then a clearer picture emerges: the dragon's scaly hide is as good as impenetrable and protects its back and upper sides. The only vulnerable parts seem to be its largely unprotected belly and lower sides – which is where Sigurd/Siegfried as well as Saint George pierce their respective dragons.[18]

The dragon is dead, yet the victorious hero will not survive him for long since the poison in his wound begins to take effect, and he dies in the knowledge of having rid his people of this menace and won for them the hoard. For Beowulf, the fight against the dragon is not only his 'chief deed', but marks both the high point and the end of a heroic life, so that the poem has been characterized correctly as

> essentially a balance, an opposition of ends and beginnings. In its simplest terms it is a contrasted description of two moments in a great life, rising and setting; an elaboration of the ancient and intensely moving contrast between youth and age, first achievement and final death.[19]

Though aesthetically pleasing, Beowulf's tragic as well as heroic end remains the exception. The dragon ranges high on any list of obstacles, yet most heroes live to tell the tale and the killing of such a monstrous foe often marks the end of a narrative cycle and the hero's promotion onto the next level rather than the end of the protagonist's life.

The career of Eglamour of Artois in the Middle English romance of the same name[20] may serve as an illustration of the dragon's main function as *maximum obstaculum*, that is, the ultimate challenge to the protagonist's strength and courage in a series of tasks. Sir Eglamour, in order to gain the hand of his beloved Christabelle, is asked by her father to fulfil three tasks of increasing difficulty:[21] first, he has to hunt one of the deer that live in a part of the forest inhabited by a giant. Eglamour succeeds in killing a hart, yet is attacked by the angry giant with an iron club. They fight till the next day and when Eglamour finally manages to cut down his opponent, he beheads him and brings the giant's head as proof of his deed to the earl – and never mind the deer. His second task, then, is to hunt down a monstrous boar[22] that has killed so many men in the area of the Kingdom of Sydon (now Lebanon) that the region is all but deserted. Sir Eglamour finds the boar easily enough, but his spear is shattered and his horse

killed, and it takes him more than three days to slay the ferocious beast. Recovering from his trials at the King of Sydon's court, he is soon challenged by yet another giant, the brother of the one he had killed during his first task, and whose pet the boar had been. Undaunted, Eglamour dons his armour and adds the defeat of the second giant to his ever-growing list of heroic exploits. Christabelle's father is, as expected, not pleased at all and, after a twenty-week respite, which Eglamour uses to get Christabelle pregnant, our hero is sent off to Rome to deal with a dragon. And indeed, Eglamour soon comes upon the dragon and the two engage in a brutal and vicious fight (lines 712–34). Eglamour cuts off half of the serpent's tongue but receives in turn a serious head wound. Yet in spite of this, he succeeds in decapitating his foe and carries the day. Fortunately Eglamour does not end like Beowulf but survives his final task, though it takes a full year of dedicated nursing care by the emperor of Rome's daughter until his health and strength are restored and he is ready for the numerous adventures ahead in the remaining 560 lines of the poem.

Sir Eglamour of Artois illustrates two points. First, the dragon, like in *Beowulf*, holds pride of place among the monstrous challengers a hero has to face.[23] The narrative principle of *post ergo difficilior* ensures that the later challenges are more difficult than the preceding ones and both *Beowulf* as a whole and the section comprising the three tasks set for Sir Eglamour are arranged accordingly. The second point, however, modifies the first one inasmuch as the dragon-slaying episode may mark the conclusion of a sequence, but no longer constitutes the end of an entire heroic career or life. This development eventually led to a situation where any hero worth his salt is expected to slay a dragon at some time or other during his chivalric career. Over time this 'proof of heroic quality' became so popular that even those protagonists who originally did not happen to kill a dragon, such as Bevis of Hampton, Lancelot or Erec, were accredited with this deed by later adaptors or translators.[24] The Old Norse adaptor-translator of Chrétien de Troyes's *Erec et Enide* (*c.*1170), for example, felt justified to insert a dragon-fight episode into his *Erex saga* (thirteenth century) after Erex's confrontation with the two giants.[25] This way the Old Norse Erex/Erec need not shun comparison with his dragon-slaying peers.

With the dragon's pride of place firmly established in the minds of the readers, new and comic potential arises – which can be found as early as the fourteenth century in the romance of *Sir Degaré*.[26] The hero has been abandoned by his mother, a princess who had been raped by a fairy knight while she was separated from her companions in the forest. Degaré is found and raised by a hermit and, at the age of twenty, he ventures forth into the world in search of his parents. In accordance with his rustic upbringing, he is armed only with a stout staff or club of oak, which proves useful when he meets an earl fighting a dragon. The beast has already devoured the earl's dogs and companions and now the earl himself is in dire straits. Degaré hastens to the earl's rescue, takes his club and beats the dragon to death:

> Ac Degarre was ful strong;
> He tok his bat, gret and long,
> And in the forehefd he him batereth

> That al the forehefd he tospatereth.
> He fil adoun anon right,
> And frapte his tail with gret might
> Upon Degarres side,
> That up-so-doun he gan to glide;
> Ac he stert up ase a man
> And with his bat leide upan,
> And al tofrusst him ech a bon,
> That he lai ded, stille as a ston.
> (*Sir Degaré*, lines 373–84)

> Yet Degaré was exceedingly strong; he took his big and long bat [club] and smote him [i.e. the dragon] on the forehead so that his forehead was bashed in completely and he fell down on the spot. And he slashed with his tail at Degaré's side so that he fell down. But up sprang Degaré and began to beat him with his club and crushed every bone so that he lay dead, still as a stone.

We cannot, of course, establish the poet's intention with absolute certainty, but I think that the poet wants to shock and amuse his audience with his youthful hero whose first deed is to beat a dragon to a pulp with a club (a non-chivalric weapon used typically by giants and wild men). As such, it is a somewhat simplistic instance of a medieval author playing with his audience's expectations, and in order to do so he makes use of two elements of dragon-lore. First, that a dragon's hide is extremely hard and thus proof against the usual attacks with lance, spear or sword. Killing a dragon by beating him to death with a club is thus a realistic option.

Secondly, that the dragon is the most dangerous of animals and occurs usually as the ultimate test for a knight's virtue and prowess. Having an inexperienced country yokel type of hero kill a dragon as his first adventure is thus a blatant violation of the norm.[27]

A more sophisticated version of such a subversion of typical romance clichés (including dragon-fights) is to be found in *Sir Gawain and the Green Knight* (late fourteenth century). When Gawain starts out from Camelot on his quest for the Green Chapel, the audience rightly expects him to encounter the usual obstacles such as giants and dragons. And though the poet sort of meets these expectations, we cannot but feel the gentle irony with which he treats these stock elements. What would take up several hundred lines in any other Middle English romance is given short shrift, and the dangers of the wild, including dragons ('wormez'), are dealt with in fewer than a dozen lines:

> Sumwhyle wyth wormez he werrez, and with
> wolues als,
> Sumwhyle wyth wodwos, that woned in the knarrez,
> Bothe wyth bullez and berez, and borez otherquyle,
> And etaynez, that hym anelede of the heye felle;[28]
> (*Sir Gawain and the Green Knight*, lines 720–3)[29]

> At whiles with worms he wars, and with wolves also,
> at whiles with wood-trolls that wandered in the crags,
> with bulls and with bears and boars, too, at times;
> and with ogres that hounded him from the heights
> of the fells.[30]

BEVIS OF HAMPTON

The Middle English romance *Bevis of Hampton* will be the focus of the second part of the chapter.[31] I have chosen this poem primarily because it contains the possibly longest autochthonous dragon episode in Middle English literature.[32] This is due to the fact that the Anglo-Norman romance *Boeve de Haumton*, which is the source for most of the Middle English text, does not contain the fight against the dragon,[33] and Bevis thus joins the ranks of all those heroes who are given a dragon-fight episode as an afterthought. Furthermore, the passage unites numerous elements from the different medieval dragon traditions and is likely to have inspired Spenser's treatment of his dragon of Eden in *The Faerie Queene* (1590/6).[34]

Yet before we turn to the dragon-fight episode proper, I would like to take a closer look at how the poet introduces the confrontation between hero and beast, and what he tells us about the provenance and origin of the worm.

The episode starts with Bevis who, after many adventures, has come to Cologne where his beloved Josian, the daughter of the King of Armenia, is baptized.[35] The narrator then continues the story:

> After Josian is cristing
> Beves dede a gret fighting,
> Swich bataile dede never non
> Cristene man of flesch ne bon,
> Of a dragoun ther be side,
> That Beves slough ther in that tide,
> Save Sire Launcelet de Lake,

> He faught with a fur drake
> And Wade dede also,
> And never knightes boute thai to,
> And Gy a Warwik, ich understonde,
> Slough a dragoun in North Homberlonde.
> (*Bevis of Hampton*, lines 2597–608)

> After Josian's christening Bevis fought a great battle. No Christian man of flesh and bone ever fought such a battle as Bevis did at that time with a nearby dragon, except Sir Lancelot du Lac – he fought with a fire drake and Wade did also. And never any knights except those two – and Sir Guy of Warwick, I believe, slew a dragon in Northumberland. (Forest-Hill, *Bevis of Hampton*, pp. 119–20)

Bevis has proved his prowess so far by killing, among others, a man-eating boar, a giant and two lions. The time has now come for him to face his dragon and thus to reach a high point of his heroic career, though luckily it will not be the end of either his life or of his adventures, which will keep the audience entertained for another 2000 lines. In order to make sure that his readers appreciate the import of this challenge, the narrator points out that the conquest of the dragon will elevate Bevis to the ranks of illustrious heroes such as Lancelot, Wade or Guy of Warwick. This meta-literary comment testifies to the poet's pronounced intertextual awareness and his endeavour to position his hero within the familiar literary landscape. The narrator then goes on to provide rather unique information about the origin of the dragon(s):

How that ilche dragoun com ther,
Ich wile yow telle, in what maner.
Thar was a king in Poyle land
And another in Calabre, ich understonde;
This twe kinge foughte ifere
More than foure and twenti yere,
That hii never pes nolde,
Naither for selver ne for golde,
And al the contré, saundoute,
Thai distruede hit al aboute;
Thai hadde mani mannes kours,
Wharthourgh hii ferden wel the wors;
Tharfore hii deide in dedli sinne
And helle pine thai gan hem winne.
After in a lite while
Thai become dragouns vile,
And so thai foughte dragouns ifere
Mor than foure and thretti yere.
(*Bevis of Hampton*, lines 2609–26)

How that dragon came to be near Cologne I will tell you. There was a king in Apulia and another in Calabria, I understand. These two kings fought each other for more than twenty-four years. They would never make peace, not for silver or gold, and all the countryside around, without doubt, they destroyed. They were cursed by many men, because of which they behaved even worse. So they died in deadly sin and won themselves hell's pain. After a little while they turned into vile dragons and so as dragons they fought together for more than thirty-four years. (Forest-Hill, *Bevis of Hampton*, p. 120)

Like Fafnir, the dragon Bevis is to face was once a man who has been transformed into this monstrous shape because of his sins.[36] This transformation due to their unrepentant and unatoned sinful behaviour is the first explicit pointer towards the strongly allegorical Christian quality of this dragon,[37] while it preserves at the same time echoes of the shape-shifting motif found in folktales and Old Norse sagas.[38] The explicit linking of the destructive warring of the two kings with the equally destructive confrontation between the two dragons would also lend itself to a socio-political interpretation as favoured for some of the folktales.[39] Proponents of such an interpretation could use the 'kings-into-dragons' section of *Bevis of Hampton* as evidence for the general (if not specific) validity of their approach since, for once, we have both sides of the equation present. However, the pre-history of the dragons contains yet another element from a different tradition. We are told that a hermit who had received Christ's mercy prayed to him for the deliverance of the people from the dragons. His wish is granted, and the two dragons depart in different directions, one settling under Saint Peter's bridge in Rome, the other beneath a cliff near Cologne (lines 2627–60). This short episode reads almost like a page out of a saint's life, though the solution of sending off the dragons far away to bother other people is reminiscent of the 'Saint Florian principle'.[40] It also foreshadows the crucial role divine assistance will play in Bevis's fight with the dragon.

The actual encounter with the dragon is preceded by two events worth commenting on. First, Bevis's double dream vision the night before his fight and, secondly,

Bevis's intention to enlist the help of the giant Ascopard. The first element is a clear instance of a 'truth' dream that is relevant to and foreshadows the events of the next day, so introducing the supernatural (divine) element.[41] The second event concerns Bevis's not unreasonable desire to enlist the help of his giant servant Ascopard, who willingly agrees to join him in the confrontation with the dragon. However, when they approach the place where the dragon dwells and hear it roar, Ascopard loses heart immediately and refuses to proceed any further, to which Bevis simply comments: 'Schame hit is, to terne aghe' (line 2758; translation: 'It is shameful to turn back').[42] Readers may condemn the giant's cowardice, but from a (medieval) narrative point of view it would be decidedly odd if we had a virtuous Christian knight and a pagan giant of doubtful moral character fighting together against the worm. The archetypal pattern requires the hero to confront the foe alone – which is the case after the giant's defection.

The dragon itself has been introduced earlier in the text by means of one of the most detailed descriptions of a dragon in medieval English literature.

> His eren were rowe and ek long,
> His frount before hard and strong;
> Eighte toskes at is mouth stod out,
> The leste was seventene ench about,
> The her, the cholle under the chin,
> He was bothe leith and grim;
> A was imaned ase a stede;
> The heved a bar with meche pride,
> Betwene the scholder and the taile

> Foure and twenti fot, saunfaile.
> His taile was of gret stringethe,
> Sextene fot a was a lingthe;
> His bodi ase a wintonne.
> Whan hit schon the brighte sonne,
> His wingges schon so the glas.
> His sides wer hard ase eni bras.
> His brest was hard ase eni ston;
> A foulere thing nas never non.
> (*Bevis of Hampton*, lines 2661–78)

> Its ears were rough and long, its face hard and strong. Eight tusks stood out from its mouth, the least was seventeen inches round. The hair and the throat under the chin were both loathsome and grim. It was maned like a horse and carried its head with great pride. Between the shoulder and the tail it was undoubtedly four and twenty foot. The tail was of great strength, sixteen feet long it was. Its body was like a wine barrel. When the bright sun shone its wings shone like glass. Its sides were hard as brass, its breast was hard as stone. There never was a fouler thing. (Forest-Hill, *Bevis of Hampton*, p. 121)

The tusks, of which the least has a circumference of some seventeen inches (that is, some 43cm),[43] connect it to the boar, while the mane on its neck links it to the horse ('stede' = 'steed'). The composite nature of the creature is further enhanced by means of its wings, which associate it with both the birds and the element of air. Furthermore, the poet develops the 'composite creature theme' through

a comparison of the dragon's torso to a wine-barrel and the association of other parts to the non-organic trilogy of glass, brass and stone. What is also striking is the accuracy of the measurements given. We are told that it measures 24 feet (7.3 metres) from shoulder to tail, with the tail another 16 feet (4.9 metres). If we add to this the neck and head, we reach a total length of approximately 14 meters – which corresponds in real-world terms to the size of a Bryde's whale (12 to 14 metres). These naturalistic elements provide a counterweight to the allegorical-spiritual aspects that gain importance after Bevis's dream vision. The realism

Illustration 15: *Bevis fighting the dragon of* Cologne. *Drawing by Anke* Eissmann.

of the monster is further enhanced by the narrator's casual reference to the 'gret stringethe' ('great strength') of the tail, which his audience is likely to have recognized as a piece of information derived from the scholarly tradition which lists the dragon's tail as its most dangerous part.[44] This is, I would argue, not the only link to the scholarly tradition. As mentioned earlier, if we jump for a moment to the end of the fight between Bevis and the dragon, we read that he cuts out the tongue of the dragon as a proof for his victory. Yet unlike Tristan, Bevis seems to have paid attention to what encyclopaedias say about dragons and their tongues, and thus avoids direct contact with it:

> And the gode knight Bevoun
> The tonge karf of the dragoun;
> Upon the tronsoun of is spere
> The tonge stikede for to bere.
> (*Bevis of Hampton*, lines 2887–90)

> The good knight Bevis carved the tongue out of the dragon. He stuck it on the shaft of his spear to carry it.
> (Forest-Hill, *Bevis of Hampton*, p. 126)

Once the stage has been set for the direct confrontation with the dragon, we are given a detailed and action-packed account of the first encounter between our hero and his foe. Bevis attacks the dragon in good chivalric tradition on his horse with his spear, which rebounds and breaks into five pieces. Undaunted, Bevis draws his sword and renews his attack and they fight till noon – which angers the dragon exceedingly:

> The dragoun was atened stronge,
> That o man him scholde stonde so longe;
> The dragoun harde him gan asaile
> And smot his hors with the taile
> Right amideward the hed,
> That he fel to grounde ded.
> (*Bevis of Hampton*, lines 2777–882)

> The dragon was infuriated that one man should withstand him so long. The dragon attacked Bevis ferociously and struck his horse with its tail right in the middle of its head so that it fell dead to the ground.
> (Forest-Hill, *Bevis of Hampton*, p. 123)

Again, the poet references the encyclopaedic tradition by having the dragon use its tail as its most potent weapon to kill Bevis's horse with a fatal blow to the head.[45] Bevis, as a consequence, finds himself without a mount and has to continue battling the monster in a less chivalric and more epic-heroic manner on foot into the night. Having been fighting for approximately ten hours or more, Bevis suffers from great thirst yet does not dare pause to drink from a nearby well. But then,

> The dragoun asailede him fot hot,
> With is taile on his scheld a smot,
> That hit clevede hevene ato,
> His left scholder dede also.
> Beves was hardi and of gode hert,
> Into the welle anon a stert.
> (*Bevis of Hampton*, lines 2796–802)

> Hot foot the dragon attacked him and hit his shield with its tail so that it split exactly in two. So did his [left] shoulder too, but Bevis was stalwart and courageous. Immediately he jumped into the well. (Forest-Hill, *Bevis of Hampton*, p. 123)

The dragon's tail proves disastrous once more and the injured hero falls into the well, which, as the narrator tells us in a short digression (lines 2803–10), has special powers due to the virgin who used to bathe in the water. It keeps the dragon away and Bevis uses the short respite to drink from the well and to invoke the aid of Saint George before he renews his attack on the dragon. The fight continues all through the night and when daylight breaks, Bevis can see things clearly again and is able to inflict a wound on the dragon ('on the dragoun hew', line 2816). However, the beast retaliates immediately and,

> The dragoun on him venim threw;
> Al ferde Beves bodi there
> A foule mesel alse yif a were;
> Thar the venim on him felle,
> His flesch gan ranclen and tebelle,
> Thar the venim was icast,
> His armes gan al to-brast;
> Al to-brosten is ventaile,
> And of his hauberk a thosend maile.
> (*Bevis of Hampton*, lines 2827–36)

> The dragon spat venom over him. All Bevis's body altered to look as if he were a foul leper. Where the

> venom fell on him his flesh began to irritate and swell. Where the venom was thrown, his armour began to break apart. His neck armour was all broken and from his chain mail shirt a thousand links fell. (Forest-Hill, *Bevis of Hampton*, pp. 124–5)

This dragon does not seem to breathe fire but spit poison, like Fafnir, who 'blew poison (eitr) over all the path before him'.[46] The effects are equally disastrous since the poison partially incapacitates Bevis and seriously damages his armour so our hero invokes Christ for assistance:

> Thanne Beves, sone an highe
> Wel loude he gan to Jesu criye:
> 'Lord, that rerede the Lazaroun,
> Dilivre me fro this fend dragoun!'
> (*Bevis of Hampton*, lines 2837–40)

> Soon Bevis began to pray very loudly to Jesus on high: 'Lord, who raised Lazarus, deliver me from this dragon-fiend.' (Forest-Hill, *Bevis of Hampton*, p. 125)

The fight against the dragon takes on more and more the quality of a conflict with the Devil, and the worm is no longer simply 'a dragoun' but 'this fend dragoun' (line 2840), that is, a demon from hell.[47] However, demon or not, our hero keeps up the struggle until the dragon's tail cleaves his helmet and basinet apart. The dragon's use of its tail as weapon links the text to the scholarly tradition, as we have seen before, yet at the same time the allegorical plot thickens. Thus, it is significant that Bevis 'Tweies a ros and tweis a fel, / The thredde tim overthrew in the wel' (lines 2849–50; translation: 'Twice he arose and twice he fell. The third time it threw him into the well' (Forest-Hill, *Bevis of Hampton*, p. 125)), which is probably a reference to Christ falling three times while carrying the cross – a motif found in popular religion.

The text now takes a decidedly allegorical turn, and parallels and analogies to biblical figures and events become quite obvious. The no more closely defined period of recovery in the water of the well is suggestive of baptism,[48] which washes away the 'poison' of sin, but it is also reminiscent of Jonah's three-day sojourn in the belly of the big fish and of Christ's three-day period in the grave. These allusions become even more pronounced once Bevis, upon regaining his strength and consciousness, invokes the help of God.

> On is knes he gan to falle,
> To Jesu Crist he gan to calle:
> 'Help,' a seide, 'Godes sone,
> That this dragoun wer overcome!
> Boute ich mowe the dragoun slon
> Er than ich hennes gon,
> Schel hit never aslawe be
> For no man in Cristenté!'
> (*Bevis of Hampton*, lines 2858–66)

> He fell on his knees and prayed again to Jesus Christ
> 'Help, God's son, so that this dragon will be overcome!
> Unless I am able to kill the dragon before I leave here it
> will never be killed by any man in Christendom!'
> (Forest-Hill, *Bevis of Hampton*, p. 125)

Bevis's prayer shows an interesting mixture of humility and heroic self-assurance. He acknowledges the fact that defeating the dragon is beyond his and any other warrior's abilities. However, with divine assistance he would be able to slay the worm and achieve what no one else could do. He thus offers himself to God as the instrument of the people's deliverance. Indeed, it is now not so much Bevis's martial prowess that is able to turn the tides in his confrontation with the dragon, but his prayer:

> To God he made his praiere
> And to Marie, his moder dere;
> That herde the dragoun, ther a stod,
> And flegh awei, ase he wer wod.
> (*Bevis of Hampton*, lines 2867–70)

> He made this prayer to God and to Mary his dear mother. The dragon heard that as it stood there and fled away as if it was mad. (Forest-Hill, *Bevis of Hampton*, p. 125)

Yet though Bevis's prayer has put the dragon to flight, *Bevis of Hampton* is not a saint's life and the narrative turns again for the greater part to the secular epic-heroic tradition for the actual killing of the dragon. Bevis chases the fleeing worm and relentlessly attacks him with his sword until he manages to split the dragon's head.

> Beves ran after, withouten faile,
> And the dragoun he gan asaile;
> With is swerd, that he out braide,

On the dragoun wel hard a laide,
And so harde a hew him than,
A karf ato his heved pan,
And hondred dentes a smot that stonde,
Er he mighte kerven a wonder,
(*Bevis of Hampton*, lines 2871–8)

Bevis ran after and began to attack it. With the sword he unsheathed he laid into the dragon and slashed at it so hard he split its skull in two. A hundred strokes he delivered at that time before he could carve out a wound.
(Forest-Hill, *Bevis of Hampton*, p. 125)

The poet does not stop here but gives a uniquely detailed description of how our hero dispatches of the dragon with almost surgical precision:

A hitte him so on the cholle
And karf ato the throte bolle.
The dragoun lai on is side,
On him a yenede swithe wide.
Beves thanne with strokes smerte
Smot the dragoun to the herte,
An hondred dentes a smot in on,
Er the heved wolde fro the bodi gon,
(*Bevis of Hampton*, lines 2879–86)

He hit it so hard in the throat he cut the Adam's apple in two. The dragon lay on its side and gaped wide at him. Bevis then with sharp strokes sliced the dragon to the heart. A hundred blows he struck in the same

> place before the head would separate from the body.
> (Forest-Hill, *Bevis of Hampton*, pp. 125–6)

As Lynn Forest-Hill argues, the 'unusual physical detail', namely Bevis's slicing through the dragon's Adam's apple ('throte bolle'), 'recalls the beast's former identity as a human with the power of speech'.[49] The theme of the (corrupting) power of speech is continued in Bevis's 'removal of the tongue [. . . which] symbolises Bevis's disarming of the Devil's ability to corrupt through speech'.[50] And indeed, as we have seen in the encyclopaedic tradition, the dragon's tongue is, next to its liver, the place where we find the highest concentration of poison. Thus, the poet uses elements from sources as different as the encyclopaedic, biblical-allegorical and epic-heroic traditions in order to create an episode that defies a simplistic reading and exploits the full interpretive potential inherent in the figure of the dragon. As a result, the 'manner of Bevis's conquest of the dragon . . . defines the parameters of hegemonically acceptable chivalric violence – against spiritual and social enemies – not for personal pride in martial prowess or love of violence'.[51]

The dragon episode in *Bevis of Hampton* constitutes something of a summa of medieval dragon lore. The poet skilfully combines factual elements rooted in the medieval encyclopaedias (tail, tongue) with the narrative role of the dragon as the *maximum obstaculum*. These two relatively realistic layers are overlaid with a spiritual one that has its roots in the biblical-allegorical tradition and that enters into a symbiotic relationship with all the other elements, exploiting their allegorical potential yet without robbing them of their factuality. As a result, we have an episode that offers multiple starting points, opens up the interpretative horizon in every direction and becomes thus the model for the more clearly allegorical dragon-fight found in Edmund Spenser's *The Faerie Queene*, which marks the transition from the Middle Ages proper to the early modern era.[52]

OUTLOOK AND CONCLUSION

THE MEDIEVAL DRAGON'S demise in the scholarly tradition with the advent of the systematic and principle-based categorization of the natural world, as found in Linnaeus's work, did not mean its complete disappearance from literature or the arts. The Christian iconographic tradition of depicting the Devil or its demonic minions as serpents or dragons kept it alive in Catholic areas, while in Protestant countries, such as post-medieval England, the surviving artwork would be reinterpreted by folklore and thus ensure the continued existence of dragon-centred narratives. There are, however, instances where the allegorical-biblical dragon has survived the secularization of modern life. Thus, it celebrates a rather surprising and unexpected comeback in, for example, the post-apocalyptic science fiction movie *Reign of Fire* (2002).

The dragon's fate in post-medieval literature and eventually film varied, depending on the degree of realism of the work. The more mimetic genres often replaced the dragon with the dinosaur, and especially the Tyrannosaurus Rex, and its somewhat less realistic relatives such as Godzilla, could be seen as the direct successors of the medieval serpent.[1] The dragon per se once more gained prominence with the re-discovery of the literature of the Middle Ages in connection with Romanticism and the rise of epic (heroic) fantasy. In this context the figure of the medievalist J. R. R. Tolkien (1892–1973), Merton Professor of English language and literature at Oxford University, and author of *The Hobbit* (1937) and *The Lord of the Rings* (1954–5), is central. Both his scholarly and literary publications have contributed considerably to the revival of the dragon in the twentieth century.[2] These continuations and adaptations of the medieval tradition by Tolkien and his predecessors, such as William Morris (1834–96), as well as his successors down to George R. R. Martin (1948–), have dominated the field of fantasy literature and related areas for a long time. It is against this background that Terry Pratchett's eighth Discworld novel *Guards! Guards!* (1989) must be read; namely as a parody of the tradition of heroic fantasy dragon-lore.

Starting at the end of the nineteenth century, we can also notice two new developments in the literary depiction of the dragon. First, there is the previously unknown phenomenon of the cuddly and harmless dragon, best represented by Kenneth Grahame's story 'The Reluctant Dragon' (1898), which derives its humour mostly from playing with the clichés of traditional dragon-lore. This development finds further representatives in figures such as Grisu, the Little Dragon (Italian original: Grisù il draghetto, 1964–75) or, as I have argued previously, in form of a parodistic inversion in Monty Python's Killer Rabbit in *Monty Python and the Holy Grail* (1975).

Secondly, we have a difficult-to-date increase in influence of the Asian (mostly Chinese) dragon, which finds its most prominent representatives in European fantasy in Falkor (German original: Fuchur) the luckdragon in Michael Ende's *The Neverending Story* (1979) and in the dragon Kalessin in Ursula K. Le Guin's Earthsea novel *Tehanu* (1990).

The Cauldron of Story has been bubbling busily over the last centuries, and continues to do so, providing the basis for the 'soup' served to a worldwide audience in different and varied forms. The dragon, whether green or any other colour, is an essential component of the cauldron's content and dragon narratives, to adapt Tolkien's words, 'must ever call with a profound appeal – until the dragon comes'.[3]

ENDNOTES

INTRODUCTION

1 Text and translation are quoted (by permission) from Benjamin Slade (ed. and trans.), *Beowulf: Diacritically Marked Text and Facing Translation*, *http://www.heorot.dk/beo-intro-rede.html*, 2002–12 (accessed 25 August 2018). All subsequent quotes and references are to this edition and translation.

2 Quoted in Tom A. Shippey, *Poems of Wisdom and Learning in Old English* (Cambridge: D.S. Brewer, 1976), pp. 76–7.

3 The Old Norse original 'Hann fnýsti eitri alla leið fyrir sik fram' (*Völsunga Saga*, ed. Guðni Jónsson and Bjarni Vilhjálmsson, *http://heimskringla.no/wiki/Völsunga_saga* (accessed 24 July 2018)) is rendered by Jesse L. Byock (ed. and trans.), *The Saga of the Volsungs* (Berkeley, CA: University of California Press, 1990), p. 63 as 'He (the dragon) blew poison (*eitr*) over all the path before him.'

4 The usually very accurate and philologically faithful translation by Gerhard Nickel gives the following version: 'Sie sahen viele *Schlangenarten* (*wyrmcynnes*) und seltsame *Seedrachen* (*sædracan*) sich überall in den Fluten tummeln sowie auf den Uferklippen *Ungeheuer* (*nicras*), *Drachen* (*wyrmas*) und *wilde Tiere* (*wildeor*) liegen, die so oft am Morgen unheilbringende Fahrten aufs Meer hinaus unternehmen.' J. Klegraf, W. Kühlwein, D. Nehls and

R. Zimmermann (eds), *Beowulf und die kleineren Denkmäler der altenglischen Heldensage Waldere und Finnsburg*. 1. *Teil: Text, Übersetzung und Stammtafeln* (Heidelberg: Carl Winter, 1976), p. 89 (italics mine).

5 Bosworth and Toller, in their *An Anglo-Saxon Dictionary*, give the following translations: *wyrmcyn*: a reptile, serpent, a creeping insect, a worm; *nicor* (pl. *nicras*): a hippopotamus, a water-monster, cf. Icelandic *nykr* = a sea goblin; a hippopotamus; OHG *nichus* = a crocodile; *sædracan*: a sea-dragon, sea-serpent; *wyrm*: a reptile, serpent (but it also means, specifically for *Beowulf* 2287ff, the fire-drake); *wildeor*: a wild beast. See Joseph Bosworth, *An Anglo-Saxon Dictionary*, ed. Thomas Northcote Toller (Oxford: At the Clarendon Press, 1898), *http://bosworth.ff.cuni.cz* (accessed 25 June 2018).

6 During his swimming contest with Brecca, Beowulf slays nine *niceras* (*Beowulf*, l. 575).

7 Semasiology is a linguistic sub-discipline that takes the word as the starting point for its inquiry into its meaning, i.e. asking 'What does X mean?' It thus stands in contrast to onomasiology that starts with the object, i.e. asking 'What is the name of X?'

8 Quoted in Bosworth, *An Anglo-Saxon Dictionary*, s.v. *hran*.

9 See Kathryn Hume, 'From Saga to Romance: The Use of Monsters in Old Norse Literature', *Studies in Philology*, 77 (1980), 1–25 and Thomas Honegger, '*Draco litterarius*: Some Thoughts on an Imaginary Beast', in Sabine Obermaier (ed.), *Tiere und Fabelwesen im Mittelalter* (Berlin and New York: Walter de Gruyter, 2009), pp. 133–45.

10 This point is beautifully illustrated in Lewis Carroll's nonsense-poem 'Jabberwocky' (in his 1871 *Through the Looking Glass, and What Alice Found There*), which seems to describe a dragon-like monstrous creature.

11 Already Edward Topsell, in his *The History of Four-footed Beasts and Serpents*, commented: 'There be some dragons which have

wings and no feet, some again have both feet and wings, and some neither feet nor wings, but are only distinguished from the common sort of Serpents by the combe growing upon their heads, and the beard under their cheeks' (Edward Topsell, *The History of Four-footed Beasts and Serpents* (London: Printed by E. Cotes, 1658), p. 705). This observation has been confirmed by Samantha Riches, who made the most comprehensive study to date of the depiction of the dragons in the Saint George tradition, and who comments on the great variety of forms in which the dragons are depicted. See Samantha J. Riches, *St George. Hero, Martyr and Myth* (Stroud: Sutton Publishing, 2000), p. 153.

12 See Qiguang Zhao, *A Study of Dragons, East and West*, Asian Thought and Culture 11 (New York: Peter Lang, 1992) for an in-depth study of the Asian and especially the Chinese dragon.

13 See also the discussion of the encyclopaedic tradition in the chapter 'The Dragon and Medieval Scholarship'.

14 Friedhelm Schneidewind, *Drachen. Das Schmöcker-Lexikon* (Saarbrücken: Verlag der Villa Fledermaus, 2008), pp. 81–5, provides a useful overview.

15 See also Carl Sagan, *The Dragons of Eden* (New York: Random House, 1977), where he argues that dragons developed out of early man's fear of reptiles in particular.

16 XII.iv.4 in Isidore of Seville, *The Etymologies of Isidore of Seville*, ed. and trans. Stephen A. Barney, W. J. Lewis, J. A. Beach and Oliver Berhof, in collaboration with Muriel Hall (Cambridge: Cambridge University Press, 2006), p. 255.

17 See, for example, the fossilized skeleton of the armoured dinosaur found by miners in Canada in 2011, *https://www.nationalgeographic.com/magazine/2017/06/dinosaur-nodosaur-fossil-discovery/* (accessed 18 July 2018).

18 See Thomas Honegger, 'From Bestiary onto Screen: Dragons in Film', in Renate Bauer and Ulrike Krischke (eds), *Fact and Fiction:*

From the Middle Ages to Modern Times. Essays Presented to Hans Sauer on the Occasion of his 65th Birthday, Texte und Untersuchungen zur Englischen Philologie 37 (Frankfurt am Main: Peter Lang, 2011), pp. 197–215, for an in-depth discussion of dragons and their modern counterparts in films.

19 See Daniel Ogden, *Dragons, Serpents, and Slayers in the Classical and Early Christian Worlds. A Sourcebook* (Oxford and New York: Oxford University Press, 2013) for an in-depth documentation of the Greek and Roman accounts of dragons and dragon-like monsters.

20 See Psalm 73 (74):13–14 and Isaiah 27:1. The lengthy poetic description of Leviathan in Job 41 characterizes it as a dragon-like creature and pays particular attention to its 'fiery' aspects: '(18) By his neesings a light doth shine, and his eyes *are* like the eyelids of the morning. (19) Out of his mouth go burning lamps, *and* sparks of fire leap out. (20) Out of his nostrils goeth smoke, as *out* of a seething pot or caldron. (21) His breath kindleth coals, and a flame goeth out of his mouth.' All quotes from and references to the Bible in English are from the critical scholarly edition of the *King James Version* (KJV) available at *https://www.academic-bible.com* (accessed 24 July 2018).

THE DRAGON AND MEDIEVAL SCHOLARSHIP

1 The table is taken from *http://en.wikipedia.org/wiki/Systema_Naturae#/media/File:Linnaeus_-_Regnum_Animale_(1735).png* (accessed 18 July 2018).

2 Topsell's work is readily available online in form of the 1658 reprint of the two volumes *The History of Four-footed Beasts* (1607) and *The History of Serpents* (1608) under the title *The History of Four-Footed Beasts* (1658) (see *https://archive.org/details/historyoffourfoo00tops* (accessed 18 July 2018)). The chapter on the dragon can be found on pp. 701–16.

3 See my entry on 'Zoology' in the *Routledge Medieval Encyclopedia Online* (forthcoming). For the development of the dragon in

zoological literature in connection with Gessner's *Schlangenbuch* ('Book on Snakes'), see the excellent study by Phil Senter, Uta Mattox and Eid E. Haddad, 'Snake to Monster: Conrad Gessner's *Schlangenbuch* and the Evolution of the Dragon in the Literature of Natural History', *Journal of Folklore Research*, 53/1 (2016), 67–124.

4 John Trevisa, *On the Properties of Things. John Trevisa's translation of Bartholomaeus Anglicus De Proprietatibus Rerum*, ed. M. Seymour et al., 3 vols (Oxford: Clarendon Press, vols I and II Text: 1975, vol. III Commentary: 1988), p. 1093.

5 The pelican is one of the birds found in the original *Physiologus*; see Otto Seel (ed. and trans.), *Der Physiologus* (Zurich: Artemis, 1992), pp. 10–11, and Michael J. Curley (ed. and trans.), *Physiologus. A Medieval Book of Nature Lore* (Chicago: The University of Chicago Press, 1979, repr. 2009), pp. 9–10.

6 Terence Hanbury White (ed. and trans.), *The Book of Beasts. Being a Translation from a Latin Bestiary of the Twelfth Century* (1st edn 1954; Stroud: Alan Sutton, 1992), pp. 132–3.

7 The concept of the Book of Nature is based upon the assumption that the created universe is as much the work of God as is the Bible – and, with the proper training, it can be 'read' (i.e. interpreted) not unlike a text from the Holy Scripture.

8 White (ed. and trans.), *The Book of Beasts*, p. 244.

9 The translation is from Augustinus, *Expositions on the Psalms*, compiled by Ted Hildebrand (online source, 2007), and the original Latin text runs as follows: 'Dicuntur hae aves tanquam colaphis rostrorum occidere parvulos suos, eosdemque in nido occisos a se lugere per triduum: postremo dicunt matrem seipsam graviter vulnerare et sanguinem suum super filios fundere, quo illi superrusi reviviscunt. Fortasse hoc verum, fortasse hoc falsum sit; tamen si verum est, quemadmodum illi congruat, qui nos vivificat sanguine suo, videte. Congruit illi quod matris caro vivificat sanguine suo filios suos: satis congruit.' The Latin original can be found in the *Enarrationes in*

Psalmos, ed. Migne, vol. III, Psalm CI, 7–8, sermo 1,8, column 1299, CCSL 40 (Turnholti, 1956).

10 One of the best-known examples of such a critical re-evaluation of traditional lore is Frederick II's *De arte venandi cum avibus* (AD *c.*1240) where he does not shy away from contrasting his own observations on the subject with what Aristotle wrote.

11 The dragon is not one of the original *Physiologus* animals but it is mentioned in the chapter on the Peridexion tree (Seel (ed. and trans.), *Physiologus*, pp. 51–2) and, arguably, the chapter on the elephant where the translation uses 'snake' (Seel (ed. and trans.), *Physiologus*, pp. 63–5; 'Schlange' = snake), which is one of the terms that can also be used to refer to the dragon.

12 See the excellent study by Bernd Roling, *Drachen und Sirenen. Die Rationalisierung und Abwicklung der Mythologie an den europäischen Universitäten* (Leiden and Boston: Brill, 2010) on some of the aspects of the dragon's afterlife.

13 Isidore (*Etymologies*, XII.iv.1–3) discusses several Latin terms for 'snake' in alphabetical order, starting with *anguis* which he derives from *angulosus*, 'turning and twisting', which is followed by *coluber* (from *colit umbras*, 'inhabits the shadows') and *serpens* (from *serpere*, 'to creep'); see Isidore of Seville, *The Etymologies of Isidore of Seville*, ed. and trans. Stephen A. Barney, W. J. Lewis, J. A. Beach and Oliver Berhof, in collaboration with Muriel Hall (Cambridge: Cambridge University Press, 2006), p. 255. Subsequent references to this text will appear in parentheses.

14 This would make Isidore a representative of the theory that sees dragons as inspired by real-world big snakes such as the python or the anaconda – although neither reaches the size to actually attack and kill an elephant, as the dragon is said to do.

15 Isidore's opening sentence will be encountered in the dragon chapter of many a bestiary (e.g. White (ed. and trans.), *The Book of Beasts*, p. 165) and encyclopaedia, even though the definition

will bring it into conflict with some of the characterizations of the dragon as a four- or two-legged creature.

16 See the discussion of Trevisa's chapter on the dragon later in this chapter for a clearer formulation of these facts.

17 See Seel (ed. and trans.), *Physiologus*, pp. 63–5, esp. p. 64.

18 Isidore (*Etymologies*, p. 251) and the earlier *Physiologus* (Seel (ed. and trans.), *Physiologus*, pp. 27–8) mention both a similar enmity between the dragon and the panther. The latter work also features the dragon as a threat to the doves that seek the protection of the tree Peridexion (cf. Seel (ed. and trans.), *Physiologus*, pp. 51–2).

19 'Cinnabar (*cinnabaris*) is named from *draco* (gen. *draconis*, "dragon") and *barrus*, that is, "elephant," for they say that it is the blood of dragons, shed when they entwine themselves around elephants. The elephants charge, and the dragons are overpowered, and the gore they shed dyes the earth, and a pigment is produced from what has stained the soil. It is a red-coloured powder' (Isidore, *Etymologies*, p. 380).

20 Isidore refers to the ever-watchful dragon that guards the golden apples of the Hesperides.

21 I use 'Trevisa' as convenient shorthand not only to refer to the English text of *On the Properties of Things* but also to refer more generally to the later medieval encyclopaedic tradition of which he is a typical representative.

22 Trevisa, *On the Properties of Things*, p. 1184. I have replaced the letters 'thorn' and 'yogh' by their equivalents 'th' and 'g/gh', respectively. Subsequent references to this text will appear in parentheses.

23 Cf. the Middle English *Sir Tristrem*: 'To bote, / His tong hath he ton / And schorn of bi the rote. / In his hose next the hide / The tong oway he bar. / No yede he bot ten stride / His speche les he thar. / Nedes he most abide / That he no may ferther far.' (Alan Lupack (ed.), *Lancelot of the Laik and Sir Tristrem*, TEAMS Middle English Series (Kalamazoo, MI: Medieval Institute Publications, 1994), p. 198, lines 1483–91). Translation: 'In addition its tongue

has he taken and cut off at the base. In his stockings, right next to his skin, he carried it away. He didn't go even ten paces when he lost the power of speech. Necessarily he must remain there and could not go any further.'

24 'And the gode knight Bevoun / The tonge karf of the dragoun; / Upon the tronsoun of is spere / The tonge stikede for to bere.' (Ronald B. Herzman, Graham Drake and Eve Salisbury (eds), *Four Romances of England. King Horn, Havelok the Dane, Bevis of Hampton, Athelston*, TEAMS Middle English Series (Kalamazoo, MI: Medieval Institute Publications, 1999), p. 277, lines 2887–90). Translation (Lynn Forest-Hill (trans.), *Bevis of Hampton* (Southampton: So: To Speak/Southampton Festivals, in association with Gumbo Press, 2015), p. 126): 'The good knight Bevis carved the tongue out of the dragon. He stuck it on the shaft of his spear to carry it …'

25 See *Beowulf*, lines 2691b–2a: '(Beowulf's) whole neck he clamped / between sharp fangs', and 2711b–15a: 'Then the wound began, / which him the earth-dragon had caused earlier, / to swelter and swell; he soon discovered that, / it him in the breast welled with deadly evil, / poison inside.' The translation is quoted (by permission) from Benjamin Slade (ed. and trans.), *Beowulf: Diacritically Marked Text and Facing Translation*, *http://www.heorot.dk/beo-intro-rede.html*, 2002–12 (accessed 25 August 2018). All subsequent quotes and references are to this edition and translation.

26 Quoted from chapter 18 of the *Völsunga saga*, ed. Guðni Jónsson and Bjarni Vilhjálmsson, *http://heimskringla.no/wiki/Völsunga_saga* (accessed 24 July 2018); and from Jesse L. Byock (ed. and trans.), *The Saga of the Volsungs* (Berkeley, CA: University of California Press, 1990), p. 93.

27 Translation: 'Also, Plinius says that because of the strength of the poison his tongue is always inflamed (or scarred), and sometimes he sets the air on fire because of the heat of the poison so that it looks as if he blows and breathes fire out of his mouth.'

28 See the chapter 'Fiery Breath' in Peter Dickinson, *The Flight of Dragons* (New York: Harper & Row, 1979), pp. 26–33. A similar 'scientific' explanation for the dragons' ability to breathe fire is given in Rob Bowman's science fiction movie *Reign of Fire* (2002).

THE DRAGON AND MEDIEVAL RELIGION

1 All quotes from and references to the Bible, be it the *King James Version* (KJV) or the *Biblia Sacra Vulgata* (*Vulgate*), are from the critical scholarly editions available at *https://www.academic-bible.com* (accessed 24 July 2018).
2 The Latin text of the *Vulgate*, which is the version relevant for the Middle Ages, has *draco* and *serpens antiquus*: '(7) et factum est proelium in caelo Michahel et angeli eius proeliabantur cum *dracone* et *draco* pugnabat et angeli eius (8) et non valuerunt neque locus inventus est eorum amplius in caelo (9) et proiectus est *draco* ille magnus *serpens antiquus* qui vocatur Diabolus et Satanas qui seducit universum orbem proiectus est in terram et angeli eius cum illo missi sunt' (italics mine).
3 Parallels to the dragon guarding the golden apples in the garden of the Hesperides in Greek mythology suggest themselves, although the snake (*serpens*) seducing Adam and Eve to eat from the fruit growing on the forbidden tree is not explicitly identified as a guardian-figure. See also the discussion of the 'snake' figure connected to the fall in Samantha J. Riches, *St George. Hero, Martyr and Myth* (Stroud: Sutton Publishing, 2000), pp. 156–8.
4 The encyclopaedists' categorization of the dragon as a snake (see the chapter 'The Dragon and Medieval Scholarship' in this study) would support such a blending of the two creatures. See also Riches, *St George*, p. 146). Riches, *St George*, p. 158, concludes: 'The "true" identity of the serpent is never made clear in textual sources, so an identification of the creature as a form of the Devil is quite permissible.'

5 The *Vulgate* renders Isaiah 27:1 as '(1) in die illo visitabit Dominus in gladio suo duro et grandi et forti super Leviathan serpentem vectem et super Leviathan serpentem tortuosum et occidet cetum qui in mari est.' *The King James Version* translates it as: '(1) In that day the Lord with his sore and great, and strong sword shall punish leviathan the piercing serpent, even leviathan that crooked serpent; and he shall slay the dragon that is in the sea.'

6 This tradition finds its echo in Milton having the fallen angels in hell turn into snakes. See John Milton, *Paradise Lost* (Book X.538ff.), available at *https://www.dartmouth.edu/~milton/reading_room/pl/book_1/text.shtml* (accessed 10 October 2018).

7 There are other *Physiologus* animals such as the phoenix whose biblical credentials are at best dubious.

8 The original *Physiologus* has a chapter on the snake (cf. Otto Seel (ed. and trans.), *Der Physiologus* (Zurich: Artemis, 1992), pp. 19–21), yet the animal discussed shares none of the characteristics of the dragon. The 'real' dragon is, however, mentioned in the chapter on the Peridexion tree (Seel (ed. and trans.), *Physiologus*, pp. 51–2) and, arguably, the chapter on the elephant where the translation uses 'snake' (Seel (ed. and trans.), *Physiologus*, pp. 63–5; 'Schlange' = snake), but which is obviously about the Isidorian dragon.

9 The bestiary paragraphs providing the allegorical interpretation often repeat the relevant information from the preceding 'scientific' description of the creature discussed. Thus for the dragon the author refers to the dragon's enormous size, to its ability to fly into the air and to ignite the air around it, to the fact that it has a crest, that its main strength is in its tail and that it lies in wait near the paths along which the elephants pass to bind their legs with its coils and to suffocate them.

10 Terence Hanbury White (ed. and trans.), *The Book of Beasts. Being a Translation from a Latin Bestiary of the Twelfth Century* (1st edn 1954; Stroud: Alan Sutton, 1992), p. 167.

11 The lion can be interpreted *in bonam partem* or *in malam partem*, depending on the context. See Paul Michel, *Tiere als Symbol und Ornament* (Wiesbaden: Ludwig Reichert Verlag, 1979), p. 46 and pp. 130–1). The interpretation *in bonam partem* takes its origin from the Lion of Judah (Genesis 49:9), that is used as an epithet to refer to Christ. This positive interpretation is also found in the *Physiologus* chapter on the lion (Seel (ed. and trans.), *Physiologus*, pp. 5–6). The interpretation *in malam partem* is based on the numerous mentions of the 'devouring lion', most prominently in 1 Petrus 5:8 (*Vulgate*): 'sobrii estote vigilate quia adversarius vester diabolus tamquam leo rugiens circuit quaerens quem devoret'; 1 Petrus 5:8 (KJV): 'Be sober, be vigilant; because your adversary the devil, as a roaring lion, walketh about, seeking whom he may devour', which explicitly identifies the 'devouring lion' as the devil. See also 2 Timothy 4:17, Psalm 21:14 (*Vulgate*) = Psalm 22:13 (KJV), Psalm 21:22 (*Vulgate*) = Psalm 22:21 (KJV), and Psalm 90:13 (*Vulgate*) = Psalm 91:13 (KJV).

12 The dragon, as part of God's creation, was originally good, and some medieval manuscript illustrations that depict Adam naming the beasts include it among the animals in Paradise. The dragon retained its positive connotation in some secular traditions, such as heraldry. See Sophie Page, 'Good Creation and Demonic Illusions: The Medieval Universe of Creatures', in Linda Kalof and Brigitte Resl (eds), *A Cultural History of Animals. Volume 2: The Medieval Age* (1000–1400) (London: Bloomsbury, 2007), pp. 27–57.

13 Riches, *St George*, p. 151, describes the situation with a slightly different emphasis: 'St Michael faced not a "real" dragon, but a creature that is explicitly said to be the Devil in the guise of a dragon; St George's foe can sometimes seem to be a representation of the Devil, but it is arguable that it often seems to be presented as a physical creature of flesh and blood.'

14 Pope Gregory the Great also advised the re-use of pagan sites in connection with the conversion of the pagan Anglo-Saxons. See his *Epistola ad Mellitum* (AD 601), preserved in Bede, *The Ecclesiastical History of the English People*, ed. and trans. Judith McClure and Roger Collins (Oxford: Oxford University Press, 1999), Book I, chapter 30, pp. 56–8.

15 Dominic Alexander, *Saints and Animals in the Middle Ages* (Woodbridge: The Boydell Press, 2008), p. 6. See also Riches, *St George*, p. 152.

16 See Riches's wide-ranging study *St George* (esp. p. 3).

17 Jacobus de Voragine, *Legenda Aurea* (*c.*1275; translated into English by William Caxton, 1483), *https://sourcebooks.fordham.edu/basis/goldenlegend/GL-vol3-george.asp* (accessed 24 July 2018).

18 See 'The Sea Monster of Ethiopia, slain by Perseus', in Daniel Ogden, *Dragons, Serpents, and Slayers in the Classical and Early Christian Worlds. A Sourcebook* (Oxford and New York: Oxford University Press, 2013), pp. 162–78, and 'The Sea Monster of Troy, slain by Heracles', in Ogden, *Dragons, Serpents, and Slayers in the Classical and Early Christian Worlds*, pp. 153–61.

19 Le Goff, in his magisterial study of Saint Marcellus (Paris), shows how the dragon that is defeated by the saint could be interpreted as a personification of the inimical forces of nature confronting the inhabitants of the area. See Jacques Le Goff, 'Ecclesiastical Culture and Folklore in the Middle Ages: Saint Marcellus of Paris and the Dragon', in Jacques Le Goff, *Time, Work, and Culture in the Middle Ages*, trans. Arthur Goldhammer (Chicago and London: The University of Chicago Press, 1980), pp. 159–88.

20 See Thomas Honegger, '*Draco litterarius*: Some Thoughts on an Imaginary Beast', in Sabine Obermaier (ed.), *Tiere und Fabelwesen im Mittelalter* (Berlin and New York: Walter de Gruyter, 2009), pp. 133–45, and Thomas Honegger, 'From Bestiary onto

Screen: Dragons in Film', in Renate Bauer and Ulrike Krischke (eds), *Fact and Fiction: From the Middle Ages to Modern Times. Essays Presented to Hans Sauer on the Occasion of his 65th Birthday*, Texte und Untersuchungen zur Englischen Philologie 37 (Frankfurt am Main: Peter Lang, 2011), pp. 197–215.

21 See Riches, *St George*, pp. 140–78, and Martin Arnold, *The Dragon. Fear and Power* (London: Reaktion Books, 2018), pp. 63–70.

22 Riches, *St George*, p. 172.

23 Riches, *St George*, p. 178.

24 *https://sourcebooks.web.fordham.edu/basis/goldenlegend/GoldenLegend-Volume4.asp#Margare* (accessed 24 July 2018).

25 The *piscis grandis* (Jonah 2:1) of the *Vulgate* is traditionally interpreted as referring to the whale, even though the text does not specify the 'big fish' any further.

26 The tradition of depicting the entrance to hell as the mouth of a dragon or a similar monster was popular throughout the Middle Ages. See, for example, the stained-glass window at Bourges Cathedral (twelfth century; 'Jaws of hell': *https://en.wikipedia.org/wiki/File:Bourges-Jaws.jpg* (accessed 24 July 2018)). The 'Harrowing of Hell' is an episode found in the apocryphal *Gospel of Nicodemus* (also known as the *Acts of Pilate*). It relates how Christ, during the three days between the crucifixion and the resurrection, descended into the realm of hell, broke open the gates of hell and led the unbaptized but virtuous and righteous pre-incarnation people such as Adam and Eve or the Old Testament patriarchs into Heaven.

27 See Le Goff's classic essay 'Ecclesiastical Culture and Folklore in the Middle Ages' on this subject.

28 See also Thomas Honegger 'The Sea-dragon – in Search of an Elusive Creature', in Gerlinde Huber-Rebenich, Christian Rohr and Michael Stolz (eds), *Wasser in der mittelalterlichen Kultur / Water in Medieval Culture* (Berlin: de Gruyter, 2017), pp. 221–31, for some further information on the theme.

29 Samantha Riches's lavishly illustrated monograph on Saint George provides many fascinating examples, yet it is not (and is not intended to be) a systematic study of the depiction of the dragon.

30 The Latin of the *Vulgate* version runs as follows: '(1) et signum magnum paruit in caelo mulier amicta sole et luna sub pedibus eius et in capite eius corona stellarum duodecim, ... (3) et visum est aliud signum in caelo et ecce draco magnus rufus habens capita septem et cornua decem et in capitibus suis septem diademata (4) et cauda eius trahebat tertiam partem stellarum caeli et misit eas in terram et draco stetit ante mulierem quae erat paritura ut cum peperisset filium eius devoraret' (*Vulgate*, Apocalipsis Iohannis 15:1, 3–4).

31 The Latin of the *Vulgate* version runs as follows: 'inimicitias ponam inter te et mulierem et semen tuum et semen illius ipsa conteret caput tuum et tu insidiaberis calcaneo eius' (Genesis 3:15).

32 The Virgin Mary is traditionally seen as the New Testament counterpart to the Old Testament Eve. The divine plan of salvation, with a good feel for symmetrical correspondences, thus enlists the help of a woman to undo the damage done by the first woman.

33 See Paul Michel, 'Was zur Beglaubigung dieser Historie dienen mag: Drachen bei Johann Jacob Scheuchzer', in Fanfan Chen and Thomas Honegger (eds), *Good Dragons are Rare. An Inquiry into Literary Dragons East and West*, ALPH 5 (Frankfurt am Main: Peter Lang, 2009), pp. 119–70, for a first overview.

34 Adolf Reinle, 'Volkskundliches in den Luzerner Kunstdenkmälern', *Schweizerisches Archiv für Volkskunde*, 51 (1955), 93–102; p. 96 dates it to 'um 1400' (*c.*1400). A black-and-white photograph of the chasuble can be found in Adolf Reinle, *Die Kunstdenkmäler des Kantons Luzern. Band* II. *Die Stadt Luzern*: I. *Teil* (Basel: Birkhäuser, 1953), p. 193.

35 See Reinle, *Die Kunstdenkmäler des Kantons Luzern*, picture 144 and p. 195.

36 See Reinle, 'Volkskundliches in den Luzerner Kunstdenkmälern', p. 96.

37 Reinle, 'Volkskundliches in den Luzerner Kunstdenkmälern', p. 95.

38 Cysat's narrative is best accessible in Reinle, 'Volkskundliches in den Luzerner Kunstdenkmälern', pp. 95–6.

39 Johann Jacob Scheuchzer (1672–1733) includes the tale in his *Naturgeschichte des Schweitzerlandes sammt seinen Reisen über die schweitzerischen Gebirge* (Zweyter Theil, pp. 228–30), which is the German translation (by Johann Georg Sulzer, 1746) of Scheuchzer's Latin original. Already he points out that the depiction on the chasuble does not tally with the description given in the tale and that the two dragons are obviously of Chinese origin.

40 Riches, *St George*, pp. 175–7, discusses this phenomenon in the Saint George tradition. See also Honegger, 'The Sea-dragon', pp. 526–7 for further examples of liberties taken by medieval authors, editors or scribes/illustrators when providing pictures for passages concerning the sea-dragon.

41 See the detailed discussion of the Asian dragon's symbolism in the study by Qiguang Zhao, *A Study of Dragons, East and West*, Asian Thought and Culture 11 (New York: Peter Lang, 1992).

42 See Michel, 'Was zur Beglaubigung dieser Historie dienen mag'. On the dragonstone in particular, see M. A. Feierabend, 'Der Luzerner Drachenstein', *Verhandlungen der Schweizerischen Naturforschenden Gesellschaft*, 46 (1862), 89–97, and, more recently, *http://www.naturmuseum.ch/home.php?sL=dau&sA=erdw&action=drac* (accessed 3 August 2018).

43 Saint George and the dragon feature not only in pageants and processions inspired by the popular saint's life, but they occur also in courtly literature, such as in Edmund Spenser's *The Faerie Queene* (1590/6).

THE MEDIEVAL DRAGON AND FOLKLORE

1 See Jacqueline Simpson, 'Fifty British Dragon Tales: An Analysis', *Folklore*, 89 (1978), 79–93, and her *British Dragons* (1980; Ware: Wordsworth, 2001); Martin Arnold, *The Dragon. Fear and Power* (London: Reaktion Books, 2018).

2 See Geoffrey of Monmouth's *Historia Regum Britanniae* (AD *c*.1136). The passage featuring the white and the red dragons is to be found in Book IV (towards the end) and continued in Book V (at the beginning).

3 See Thomas Honegger, 'The Man in the Moon: Structural Depth in Tolkien', in Thomas Honegger (ed.), *Root & Branch: Approaches towards Understanding Tolkien* (1999; Zurich and Berne: Walking Tree Publishers, 2005), pp. 9–70, for a comprehensive presentation and analysis of the extant textual and pictorial evidence.

4 I use 'text' in the widest sense of the word, which includes not only written texts, but also oral narratives and the products of the pictorial and performative arts.

5 Le Goff, in his study of Saint Marcellus and the dragon of Paris, has gathered evidence for the use of dragon effigies in Rogation Day processions and similar events during the Middle Ages. See Jacques Le Goff, 'Ecclesiastical Culture and Folklore in the Middle Ages: Saint Marcellus of Paris and the Dragon', in Jacques Le Goff, *Time, Work, and Culture in the Middle Ages*, trans. Arthur Goldhammer (Chicago and London: The University of Chicago Press, 1980), pp. 159–88.

6 Alexander Neckam (1157–1217), in chapter XIV ('De macula lunae', i.e. 'About the mark/blemish of the moon') of the first book of his treatise *De Naturis Rerum* (see Alexander Neckam, *De naturis rerum libri duo*, ed. Thomas Wright, Rolls Series 34 (London: Longman, Green, Longman, Roberts and Green, 1863), pp. 53–4) discusses the various theories concerning the origin and nature of the 'shadow' or 'mark' on the moon. He also

mentions the Man in the Moon and asks his readers rhetorically: 'Nonne novisti quid vulgus vocet rusticum in luna portantem spinas?' (i.e. 'Don't you know that which the common crowd calls "The peasant in the moon, who carries thorns"?') Neckam thus places the Man in the Moon clearly into the realm of folklore ('quid vulgus vocet').

7 Andrew Lang (ed.), *The Red Fairy Book* (4th edn; London: Longmans, Green & Co., 1893), p. 357.

8 See J. R. R. Tolkien's *Beowulf. A Translation and Commentary together with Sellic Spell*, ed. Christopher Tolkien (London: HarperCollins, 2014) for a similar project with his *Sellic Spell* for the first part of the Old English epic *Beowulf*. See Thomas Honegger, 'Transformations of Fairy Stories: From *Sellic/Sælig Spell* to *Beowulf*, or from Folk Tale to Epic', *Hither Shore*, 12 (2016), 248–60 for a detailed discussion of Lang's and Tolkien's achievements respectively.

9 Lays are short (typically 600–1000 lines), rhymed tales that deal with matters of love or chivalry, often involving elements of the supernatural. The plot is usually limited to a single strand of action, in contrast to romances, which typically comprise multiple (parallel) sub-narratives.

10 J. R. R. Tolkien, *Tolkien On Fairy-stories*, ed. Verlyn Flieger and Douglas A. Anderson (London: HarperCollins, 2008), pp. 44–5.

11 See Karl Shuker, *Dragons: A Natural History* (New York: McGraw-Hill, 1995), pp. 48–51, p. 51.

12 Devlin was a self-educated journeyman and shoemaker with a strong interest in (local) history. He published on the shoemaker's and other trades and miscellaneous other topics; James Dacres Devlin, *The Mordiford Dragon, to which is added The Priest, Lady, and Bailiff; a tale of Hereford of the time of the Conquest: as also, The Verses on the Aged 'Aunt Bess'* (Hereford: Printed by C. Anthony, Widemarsh-Street, 1848). Subsequent references to this text will appear in parentheses.

13 It is very likely that Devlin is actually referring to himself when he talks about his trustworthy 'informant'.

14 See Shuker, *Dragons*, p. 48. The wyvern's main characteristics are his two (short) legs and two wings.

15 Contemporary readers will notice the intertextual parallels to, for example, Daenerys Stormborn, the Mother of Dragons, in George Martin's *A Song of Ice and Fire*, or to J. K. Rowling's Hagrid, who, in *Harry Potter and the Philosopher's Stone*, hatches a dragon's egg and tries to raise the fast-growing baby dragon – with rather comical-disastrous results.

16 Devlin, *The Mordiford Dragon*, p. 32 identifies the convict in his 'historical preface' as the 'Garston' mentioned in the inscription that accompanied the depiction of the serpent in the church.

17 Devlin must have added this detail, maybe remembering and contrasting it to Tristan's less fortunate encounter with the tongue of his dragon. Or it is an instance of a Cauldron of Story ingredient popping up in very different types of soup.

18 The passage relating the fight between Winckelried and the dragon is quoted in full in Paul Michel, 'Was zur Beglaubigung dieser Historie dienen mag: Drachen bei Johann Jacob Scheuchzer', in Fanfan Chen and Thomas Honegger (eds), *Good Dragons are Rare. An Inquiry into Literary Dragons East and West*, ALPH 5 (Frankfurt am Main: Peter Lang, 2009), pp. 119–70, here p. 126. Winckelried also makes an appearance in Shuker's anthology in the story of 'The Dragonet of Mount Pilatus' (Shuker, *Dragons*, pp. 74–5).

19 The tale has its origins in the early decades of the twentieth century but the fully revised and unified version was published only posthumously by Christopher Tolkien in 2007; see J. R. R. Tolkien, *The Children of Húrin*, ed. Christopher Tolkien (London: HarperCollins, 2007). The cursed hero Túrin Turambar fights and kills the dragon Glaurung yet, like Tristan, swoons from the effects of the dragon's poisonous blood.

20 Samuel Ireland, *Picturesque Views on the River Wye* (London: Published by R. Faulder, New Bond Street; and T. Egerton, Whitehall, 1797), pp. 60–2.

21 George Lipscombe, *Journey into South Wales, through the counties of Oxford, Warwick, Worcester, Hereford, Salop, Stafford, Buckingham, and Hertford; in the year* 1799 (London: Printed by A. Strahan, Printers Street, for T. N. Longman & O. Rees, Paternoster Row, 1802), pp. 71–2. Subsequent references to this text will appear in parentheses.

22 Shuker, *Dragons*, p. 50, provides a small reproduction of Mordiford church with a large painting of a wyvern on its wall, yet fails (as usual) to provide any information on the origin of the picture.

23 Arnold, *The Dragon. Fear and Power*, p. 176, writes that 'the lords of the manor in Mordiford in the seventeenth and eighteenth centuries were the Garstons, whose family crest depicted a great wyvern'. James Fairbairn, *Fairbairn's Book of Crests of the Families of Great Britain and Ireland*, 2 vols (1859; 4th, rev. and expanded edn; London: TC & EC Jack, 1905), vol. 1, p. 221, describes the Garston crest as follows: 'Garston, out of a mural coronet arg(ent), a wyvern or, charged on the breast with a fire-ball sa(ble).' This suggests that the Garstons adopted the wyvern for their crest as a reference to the folktale and that, as a consequence, the wyvern depicted on the church may have been connected to the heraldic symbolism of that family.

24 Devlin, *The Mordiford Dragon*, p. 38, dates the destruction to between 1810 and 1812. See also Devlin's detailed discussion of the painting and its mention in various sources (*The Mordiford Dragon*, pp. 40–7).

25 The only dragon that meets its end at the hands of an angry crowd is, to the best of my knowledge, the Tarasque. And this is probably only possible since it occurs in a saint's life and not in an epic.

26 See Jesse L. Byock (ed. and trans.), *The Saga of the Volsungs* (Berkeley, CA: University of California Press, 1990), p. 63.

27 Arnold, *The Dragon*, pp. 171–89.

28 Arnold, *The Dragon*, p. 177.

29 See J. R. R. Tolkien's landmark 1936 British Academy lecture 'Beowulf: The Monsters and the Critics' (in J. R. R. Tolkien, *The Monsters and the Critics and Other Essays*, ed. Christopher Tolkien (London: HarperCollins, 1997), pp. 5–48.), where he points out the aesthetic-structural balance achieved by juxtaposing the account of the young Beowulf's exploits in the first part of the poem with the aged hero's final battle against the dragon in the second half.

30 It is Shuker's retelling that seems to have become the canonical version – at least if we judge by its popularity on the Internet (see, for example, *https://en.wikipedia.org/wiki/Dragon_of_Mordiford*, or *https://princessofdragons.wordpress.com/2014/10/17/the-mordiford-wyvern/* (accessed 24 July 2018)).

31 J. R. R. Tolkien, *The Letters of J. R. R. Tolkien*, ed. Humphrey Carpenter, with the assistance of Christopher Tolkien (1981; Boston: Houghton Mifflin, 2000), p. 214.

32 J. R. R. Tolkien, 'The Dragon's Visit', *Oxford Magazine* 55/1 (4 February 1937), 342.

THE DRAGON AND MEDIEVAL LITERATURE

1 I use the term 'literature' in order to refer to the fictional texts written for an educated though not primarily clerically trained target audience and indebted to a largely secular ethos. 'Literature' in this sense differs thus from the (in its origin) oral folk-literature as well as from the religious and scholarly scientific texts.

2 Text and translation are quoted (by permission) from Benjamin Slade (ed. and trans.), *Beowulf: Diacritically Marked Text and Facing*

Translation, *http://www.heorot.dk/beo-intro-rede.html*, 2002–12 (accessed 25 August 2018). All subsequent quotes and references are to this edition and translation.

3 I say 'erroneously' since neither England nor any Englishmen (or Anglo-Saxons) play a role in the entire poem, which takes place mostly in southern Sweden, Denmark and parts of northern Germany. It is, however, written in Old English.

4 See, most recently, Tom Shippey's equally competent and readable chapter 'Hygelac and Hrolf: False Dawn for the Viking', in *Laughing Shall I Die. Lives and Deaths of the Great Vikings* (London: Reaktion Books, 2018), pp. 38–62, in which he discusses the often very complex and entangled situation in fifth- and sixth-century Scandinavia. It is the events in this Dark Age period that provide much of the background for the setting in *Beowulf*.

5 J. R. R. Tolkien, professor of Anglo-Saxon at Oxford, was inspired by this episode for his depiction of Bilbo's theft of the golden cup from Smaug's hoard and the dragon's subsequent rage in *The Hobbit* (1937).

6 Theories positing a Fafnir-like transformation of this 'last survivor' into the dragon must remain speculations. The text itself does not mention such a transformation.

7 Even Peter Jackson, in the prologue to his movie *The Hobbit: An Unexpected Journey* (2013) narrating Smaug's attack on Erebor, seems to imply that one should not pile up too much treasure in one place.

8 *Maxims* II (lines 26b–7a) read: 'Draca sceal on hlæwe, / frod, frætwum wlanc.' (Translation: 'A dragon must live in a barrow, / old and proud of his treasures.') Tom A. Shippey, *Poems of Wisdom and Learning in Old English* (Cambridge: D.S. Brewer, 1976), pp. 76–7.

9 I use the term '*Beowulf*-poet' to refer to the writer who gave the poem the form we have in front of us today. It is very likely that he used older elements that, possibly, had their origins in pagan Germanic tradition.

10 The very last word in the extant text of *Beowulf* is an adjective describing the deceased hero as *lofgeornost*, i.e. 'most eager for fame'. A discussion of its connection to 'Northern courage' would exceed the limits of this study. See, however, J. R. R. Tolkien, 'Beowulf: The Monsters and the Critics', in J. R. R. Tolkien, *The Monsters and the Critics and Other Essays*, ed. Christopher Tolkien (London: HarperCollins, 1997), pp. 5–48, here pp. 25–6, for a brief characterization of this attitude.

11 'oferhogode' is the third person singular preterite form of *ofer-hycgan*.

12 See Helmut Gneuss, '*The Battle of Maldon* 89: Byrhtnoð's *ofermod* Once Again', in Katherine O'Brien O'Keeffe (ed.), *Old English Shorter Poems: Basic Readings* (New York and London: Garland Publishing, 1994), pp. 149–72, and Paul Cavill, 'Interpretation of *The Battle of Maldon*, Lines 84–90: A Review and Reassessment', *Studia Neophilologica*, 67 (1995), 149–64, for a detailed discussion of *ofermod* and its implications.

13 This pattern is still going strong. Thus, the 2002 movie *Reign of Fire* presents a post-apocalyptic scenario with dragons ruling the world. Yet in the end we have a showdown between one man and one dragon.

14 Tolkien, 'Beowulf: The Monsters and the Critics', p. 16.

15 I have taken Beowulf's shout challenging the dragon as the beginning of the conflict proper, which ends with the death of the dragon (*Beowulf*, lines 2550–709a). However, I have not counted the digressions and parallel events that are not directly connected to the fighting.

16 Beowulf takes along eleven companions, with the cup-thief to show them the way.

17 See, for example, Paul Acker, 'Dragons in the Eddas and in Early Nordic Art', in Paul Acker and Carolyne Larrington (eds), *Revisiting the Poetic Edda. Essays on Old Norse Heroic Legend* (New York and London: Routledge, 2013), pp. 53–75. These sources, such

as Sigurd's fight against Fafnir, have admittedly been preserved only in documents and carvings that post-date *Beowulf*, yet they seem to testify to and preserve a much older (common Germanic) tradition.

18 Illustrations of these fights can be found in Acker, 'Dragons in the Eddas and in Early Nordic Art', for Sigurd, and Samantha J. Riches, *St George. Hero, Martyr and Myth* (Stroud: Sutton Publishing, 2000), for Saint George.

19 Tolkien, 'Beowulf: The Monsters and the Critics', p. 28.

20 All references are to the edition by Harriet Hudson (ed.), *Four Middle English Romances: Sir Isumbras, Octavian, Sir Eglamour of Artois, Sir Tryamour*, TEAMS Middle English Series (Kalamazoo, MI: Medieval Institute Publications, 2006), accessible at *http://d.lib.rochester.edu/teams/text/hudson-sir-eglamour-of-artois* (accessed 14 August 2018).

21 The motif of an unwilling father of the bride who wants to prevent the marriage by setting (impossible) tasks to the suitor is widespread and can be found, for example, in the Welsh romance *Culhwch and Olwen* (*c.*1100) and again in J. R. R. Tolkien's *Beren and Lúthien*.

22 Killing the Erymanthian Boar was Hercules' fourth labour.

23 This is also corroborated by Bevis of Hampton who, upon sighting his monstrous opponent exclaims: 'Hadde we the dragoun wonne, / We hadde the feireste pris under sonne!' Ronald B. Herzman Graham Drake and Eve Salisbury (eds), *Four Romances of England. King Horn, Havelok the Dane, Bevis of Hampton, Athelston*, TEAMS Middle English Series (Kalamazoo, MI: Medieval Institute Publications, 1999), lines 2745–6. All references to the Middle English text are to this edition. Translation: 'If we defeat it we will have the fairest prize under the sun!' All translations of *Bevis* are quoted (by permission) from Lynn Forest-Hill (trans.), *Bevis of Hampton* (Southampton: So: To Speak/Southampton Festivals, in association with Gumbo Press, 2015), here p. 122.

24 Bevis (or Boeve), in the older Anglo-Norman version, is no dragon-slayer – nor are Lancelot or Erec in Chrétien's romances.

25 See chapter 10 in Foster W. Blaisdell Jr. and Marianne E. Kalinke (trans.), *Erex Saga and Ívens Saga. The Old Norse Versions of Chrétien de Troyes's Erec and Yvain* (Lincoln and London: University of Nebraska Press, 1977), here pp. 22–5.

26 All references are to the edition by Anne Laskaya and Eve Salisbury (eds), *The Middle English Breton Lays*, TEAMS Middle English Text Series (Kalamazoo, MI: Medieval Institute Publications, 1995), accessible at *http://d.lib.rochester.edu/teams/text/laskaya-and-salisbury-middle-english-breton-lays-sir-degare* (accessed 16 August 2018).

27 The non-chivalric method of fighting against the dragon is just one of the numerous folktale elements in this romance.

28 The letters 'yogh' and 'thorn' have been replaced by their modern equivalents.

29 Quoted from the edition by J. R. R. Tolkien and Eric Valentine Gordon (eds), *Sir Gawain and the Green Knight*, 2nd edn, ed. Norman Davies (1925; Oxford: Clarendon Press, 1967), p. 20.

30 Quoted from J. R. R. Tolkien (trans.), *Sir Gawain and the Green Knight, Pearl, and Sir Orfeo*, ed. Christopher Tolkien (1975; London: HarperCollins, 1995), p. 38.

31 All references are to the edition by Herzman et al. (eds), *Four Romances of England*, accessible at *http://d.lib.rochester.edu/teams/text/salisbury-four-romances-of-england-bevis-of-hampton* (accessed 16 August 2018). See also the most recent critical edition by Jennifer Fellows, *Bevis of Hampton*, 2 vols, Early English Text Society Original Series 349 and 350 (Oxford: Oxford University Press, 2017), which considers a greater number of manuscripts.

32 Judith Weiss, 'The Major Interpolations in *Sir Beues of Hamtoun*', *Medium Ævum*, 48 (1979), 71–6, 72, calls it 'one of the earliest and most original dragon-fights in English mediaeval romance'. See also Nicolas Jacobs, '*Sir Degarré*, *Lay le Freine*, *Beves of Hamtoun*,

and the "Auchinleck Bookshop"', *Notes and Queries*, 227 (1982), 294–301, esp. 297–301, who analyses the relationship between the dragon episodes in *Bevis of Hampton* and *Sir Degaré*, and who argues in favour of the primacy of the dragon episode in *Bevis*.

33 See Weiss, 'The Major Interpolations in *Sir Beues of Hamtoun*', and Jacobs, '*Sir Degarré, Lay le Freine, Beves of Hamtoun*, and the "Auchinleck Bookshop"', for a discussion of the interpolation. The entire dragon-fight episode can be found in *Bevis of Hampton*, lines 2597–910 (pp. 269–77). See also the dragon episodes in other manuscripts of Bevis, as found in the edition by Fellows, *Bevis of Hampton*, pp. 184–99 and in appendix 5, pp. 294–302.

34 See Andrew King, *The Faerie Queene and Middle English Romance: The Matter of Just Memory* (Oxford: Clarendon Press, 2000), pp. 129–45, on the connection between the dragon-fight episodes in *Bevis of Hampton* and *The Faerie Queene*. See Jennifer Fellows, '"Dragons two other thre": The Dragon Motif in Some Middle English Romances' (unpublished manuscript), 2–5, on the connection between the dragon episode in *Bevis* and other Middle English romances.

35 For a convenient and succinct summary of the story, see the 'Introduction' to the text in Herzman et al. (eds), *Four Romances of England*, pp. 190–6, also accessible at *http://d.lib.rochester.edu/teams/text/salisbury-bevis-of-hampton-introduction* (accessed 16 August 2018).

36 With Fafnir it is arguably *avaritia* ('greed') that causes the transformation, while in the case of the two kings it is probably *ira* ('anger, wrath'). The idea of greed turning a human into a dragon has been taken up by C. S. Lewis in his *The Voyage of the Dawn Treader* (1952), where Eustace transforms into a dragon when he begins to covet the hoard he has found in a deserted cave.

37 Fellows, '"Dragons two other thre": The Dragon Motif in Some Middle English Romances', 5, argues that 'the function of this episode seems entirely symbolic, since it is a completely

detachable one with no narrative consequences' and provides an in-depth interpretation of this episode in the subsequent pages of her paper.

38 See, for example, Bödvar Bjarki in the *Saga of Hrolf Kraki*, though he does not really shapeshift but sends a kind of 'fetch' in the form of a gigantic bear while his human body remains unconscious or asleep. For a discussion of instances of human-to-dragon metamorphoses in Old Norse literature, see Robert E. Cutrer, 'The Wilderness of Dragons. The Reception of Dragons in Thirteenth-century Iceland' (unpublished MA thesis, University of Iceland, 2012), 25–7. The dragons of the Asian tradition can take on the shape of humans, while this seems to be not the case in the Western tradition – with the exception of the dragon in chapter 9 of the *Morkinskinna*. We are told that during his stay at the court of Constantinople, Haraldr Hardraada helped to unmask the mysterious lover of the wife of one of his men as a shape-shifting dragon (Theodore M. Andersson and Kari Ellen Gade (trans. and eds), *Morkinskinna. The Earliest Icelandic Chronicle of the Norwegian Kings* (1030–1157), Islandica 51 (Ithaca and London: Cornell University Press, 2000), esp. pp. 133–4). It may be no coincidence that this adventure takes place in Constantinople, which has traditionally been the gateway to the East.

39 See Martin Arnold, *The Dragon. Fear and Power* (London: Reaktion Books, 2018), pp. 171–89, for some exemplary socio-political interpretations of folktales featuring dragons. See also Shippey's perspicuous comments on the attempts (mostly by German scholars) to interpret the fight between Sigurd and Fafnir as an allegory of Arminius's victory over the Roman legions in AD 9 in the Kalkriese region (Shippey, *Laughing Shall I Die*, p. 66).

40 The Saint Florian Principle (German *Sankt Florians Prinzip*) derives its name from the somewhat ironic invocation of the saint with

the words: 'Oh Holy Saint Florian, please spare my house and have the fire consume another one!'

41 The dream-vision(s) sequence covers lines 2681 to 2690. For dreams and dream-visions, see Spearing's classic study on medieval dream poetry: A. C. Spearing, *Medieval Dream-Poetry* (Cambridge: Cambridge University Press, 1976).

42 Bevis exhibits a courage and determination similar to many (medieval) heroes who stick to their original purpose in spite of daunting odds.

43 The nature of medieval measurements varies not only with time but also from region to region. I therefore use the modern standard measurements as an approximation.

44 See also the information given in chapter 13 of the *Morkinskinna* where Haraldr suggests that 'Ulfr is the strongest so he should attack the tail, as that is where serpents have their power' (Paul Acker (trans.), 'The Dragon Episode in *Morkinskinna*', ANQ: *A Quarterly Journal of Short Articles, Notes, and Reviews*, 20/3 (2007), 65–8, here 66).

45 Bevis's fight against the dragon of Cologne shows numerous parallels to the shorter description relating Sir Tristram's encounter with the dragon of Ireland in *Sir Tristrem* (see Alan Lupack (ed.), *Lancelot of the Laik and Sir Tristrem*, TEAMS Middle English Series (Kalamazoo, MI: Medieval Institute Publications, 1994), pp. 197–8, lines 1440–85), though there are also important differences.

46 Jesse L. Byock (ed. and trans.), *The Saga of the Volsungs* (Berkeley, CA: University of California Press, 1990), p. 63.

47 *fend* used in the meaning of 'enemy' is last attested in the *Ayenbite of Inwyt* (1340). The meaning 'demon' or 'devil' is attested from Old English to Modern English. Allusions to the 'hellish' nature of dragons may work as simple metaphorical embellishment and need not necessarily be interpreted literally all the time. They do evoke, however, the allegorical

potential of the encounter. See, for example, Sir Tristrem's encounter with the dragon that greets him with 'Helle-fere' (Lupack (ed.), *Lancelot of the Laik and Sir Tristrem*, p. 197, line 1440; translation: 'hell-fire') and is further given the epithet 'devel' in 'The devel dragouns hide' (Lupack (ed.), *Lancelot of the Laik and Sir Tristrem*, p. 197, line 1451; translation: 'The fiendish dragon's hide').

48 See Lynn Forest-Hill, 'Fantasy Elements in Medieval Romance: History or Imagination?', *Yearbook of Eastern European Studies*, 6 (2016), 61–76, here 66, for a discussion of the Christian spiritual elements of this scene.

49 Forest-Hill, 'Fantasy Elements in Medieval Romance', 68.

50 Forest-Hill, 'Fantasy Elements in Medieval Romance', 68.

51 Forest-Hill, 'Fantasy Elements in Medieval Romance', 69.

52 See Maik Goth, 'Spenser's Dragons', in Fanfan Chen and Thomas Honegger (eds), *Good Dragons are Rare. An Inquiry into Literary Dragons East and West*, ALPH 5 (Frankfurt am Main: Peter Lang, 2009), pp. 97–117. The relevant passage is to be found in *The Faerie Queene*, book 1, cantos xi and xii. Spenser's Red Crosse Knight who, as the representative of the Anglican Church, fights against the dragon (=Satan) not merely in the traditional epic manner with lance and sword but also, or even more so, with spiritual means. Both the anonymous poet of the Middle English *Bevis of Hampton* and, in his wake, Spenser thus allegorizes the epic and romance traditions which often feature the dragon as the ultimate opponent for the hero and thus provide a link between the hagiographic and the secular traditions. Even the epic division between secular worm and allegorical dragon is not always consistently kept and romance may turn into saint's life, as can be seen in *Guy of Warwick* whose eponymous hero, in the second part of the romance, becomes a pilgrim, a warrior for Christ and, in the end, a (saintly) hermit.

OUTLOOK AND CONCLUSION

1 See Thomas Honegger, 'From Bestiary onto Screen: Dragons in Film', in Renate Bauer and Ulrike Krischke (eds), *Fact and Fiction: From the Middle Ages to Modern Times. Essays Presented to Hans Sauer on the Occasion of his 65th Birthday*, Texte und Untersuchungen zur Englischen Philologie 37 (Frankfurt am Main: Peter Lang, 2011), pp. 197–215, for an in-depth discussion of this aspect of the dragon's afterlife in modern film.

2 See his British Academy lecture 'Beowulf: The Monsters and the Critics' (1936) and the dragons in *The Hobbit* (1937) as well as in *Farmer Giles of Ham* (1949).

3 J. R. R. Tolkien, 'Beowulf: The Monsters and the Critics', in J. R. R. Tolkien, *The Monsters and the Critics and Other Essays*, ed. Christopher Tolkien (London: HarperCollins, 1997), pp. 5–48, here p. 34.

FURTHER READING

(SELECTIVE ANNOTATED BIBLIOGRAPHY)

The following books (in alphabetical order by author) are recommended reading for all interested in dragons, medieval and beyond.

Arnold, Martin, *The Dragon. Fear and Power* (London: Reaktion Books, 2018): Arnold's book is not only the most recent one, it is also the most comprehensive study covering dragons East and West as well as old and new. Arnold, formerly senior lecturer in English at the University of Hull, has a talent for combining high-quality academic research with a general accessibility and readability. The book is lavishly illustrated and offered at a bargain price. Highly recommended.

Kordecki, Lesley Catherine, 'Traditions and Development of the Medieval English Dragon' (unpublished PhD thesis, University of Toronto, Centre for Medieval Studies, 1980): Kordecki's thesis is, unfortunately, not readily available and only accessible via interlibrary copy order (from microfiche). After a theoretical part on the function of monsters (and the dragon in particular) in the Middle Ages and an overview on the dragon's origin in ancient mythologies, she provides an illuminating discussion of the dragon in the different genres of medieval English literature (saints' lives, romances and *Beowulf*). The study is of interest for those academic researchers dealing with the dragon specifically in medieval English literature.

Ogden, Daniel, *Dragons, Serpents, and Slayers in the Classical and Early Christian Worlds. A Sourcebook* (Oxford and New York: Oxford University Press, 2013): Ogden's volume is an indispensable source for all the texts of classical antiquity central to the dragon theme. These are complemented by the most important dragon-related narratives from the biblical tradition and medieval saints' lives. Not a book to be read cover to cover but highly recommended for its faithful translations of important Greek and Latin source texts.

Petty, Anne C., *Dragons of Fantasy* (2nd edn; Crawfordville FL: Kitsune Books, 2008): Petty's study is of interest for all those who would like to explore the afterlife of the medieval dragon in the works of fantasy literature. The volume covers dragons in J. R. R. Tolkien, Anne McCaffrey, Terry Pratchett, Ursula K. Le Guin, Jane Yolen, Terry Goodkind and J. K. Rowling.

Simpson, Jacqueline, *British Dragons* (1980; Ware: Wordsworth, 2001): this is the classic study on dragons in British folklore. Essential reading for all interested in British dragons.

Steer, Dugald A. (ed.), *Dr. Ernest Drake's Dragonology. The Complete Book of Dragons* (Somerville, MA: Candlewick Press, 2003): this richly illustrated volume is lovingly equipped with special features and will fascinate not only young readers, for whom it has been primarily designed. It is an attractive and well-made representative of the *faux* science genre.

Zhao, Qiguang, *A Study of Dragons, East and West*, Asian Thought and Culture 11 (New York: Peter Lang, 1992): Zhao's book is, next to de Visser's classic study on the Asian dragon, the only academic monograph that investigates the Eastern tradition in depth – and compares and contrasts it to the Western tradition. Essential reading for all interested in the non-European dragon.

BIBLIOGRAPHY

Acker, Paul (trans.), 'The Dragon Episode in *Morkinskinna*', ANQ: *A Quarterly Journal of Short Articles, Notes, and Reviews*, 20/3 (2007), 65–8.

——, 'Dragons in the Eddas and in Early Nordic Art', in Paul Acker and Carolyne Larrington (eds), *Revisiting the Poetic Edda. Essays on Old Norse Heroic Legend* (New York and London: Routledge, 2013), pp. 53–75.

Alamichel, Marie-Françoise, 'De *Beowulf* à Malory: Les dragons dans la littérature médiévale anglaise', in Danielle Buschinger and Wolfgang Spiewok (eds), *Le dragon dans la culture médiévale*, Wodan 39 (Greifswald: Reineke-Verlag, 1994), pp. 1–10.

Alban, Gillain M. E., 'The Serpent Goddess Melusine: From Cursed Snake to Mary's Shield', in Paul Hardwick and David Kennedy (eds), *The Survival of Myth: Innovation, Singularity and Alterity* (Newcastle upon Tyne: Cambridge Scholars Publishing, 2010), pp. 23–43.

Alexander, Dominic, *Saints and Animals in the Middle Ages* (Woodbridge: The Boydell Press, 2008).

Andersson, Theodore M. and Kari Ellen Gade (trans. and eds), *Morkinskinna. The Earliest Icelandic Chronicle of the Norwegian Kings*

(1030–1157), Islandica 51 (Ithaca and London: Cornell University Press, 2000).

Arduini, Roberto, '"Non farti mai beffe di un drago vivo, pazzo di un Bilbo!" Il revival medieval dei Draghi di J.R.R. Tolkien', in Roberto Arduini, Alberto Ladavas and Saverio Simonelli (eds), *C'era una volta … Lo Hobbit. Alle origini del Signore degli Anelli* (Genoa and Milan: Marietti 1820, 2012), pp. 180–206.

Arnold, Martin, *The Dragon. Fear and Power* (London: Reaktion Books, 2018).

Augustine, *City of God*, trans. David S. Wiesen, vol. III, books 8–11 (Harvard: Harvard University Press, 1968).

—, *Expositions on the Psalms*, compiled by Ted Hildebrand (online source, 2007).

Baring, Anne and Jules Cashford, *The Myth of the Goddess: Evolution of an Image* (London: Penguin, 1991).

Bede, *The Ecclesiastical History of the English People*, ed. and trans. Judith McClure and Roger Collins (Oxford: Oxford University Press, 1999).

Bible, Biblia sacra Vulgata and King James Version, *https://www.academic-bible.com* (accessed 24 July 2018).

Bildhauer, Bettina and Robert Mills (eds), *The Monstrous Middle Ages* (Cardiff: University of Wales Press, 2003).

Blaisdell Jr., Foster W. and Marianne E. Kalinke (trans.), *Erex Saga and Ívens Saga. The Old Norse Versions of Chrétien de Troyes's Erec and Yvain* (Lincoln and London: University of Nebraska Press, 1977).

Blust, Robert, 'The Origin of Dragons', *Anthropos: International Review of Anthropology and Linguistics*, 95/2 (2000), 519–36.

Bonjour, Adrien, 'Monsters Crouching and Critics Rampant: Or the Beowulf Dragon Debated', in Adrien Bonjour, *Twelve Beowulf Papers* (Neuchâtel: Faculté des Lettres, 1962), pp. 97–113.

Bosworth, Joseph, *An Anglo-Saxon Dictionary*, ed. Thomas Northcote Toller (Oxford: At the Clarendon Press, 1898), *http://bosworth.ff.cuni.cz* (accessed 25 June 2018).

Brall-Tuchel, Helmut, 'Drachen und Drachenkämpfe in Geschichtsschreibung, Legende und Roman des Mittelalters', *Saeculum*, 57/2 (2006), 213–30.

Buschinger, Danielle and Wolfgang Spiewok (eds), *Le dragon dans la culture médiévale*, Wodan 39 (Greifswald: Reineke-Verlag, 1994).

Byock, Jesse L. (ed. and trans.), *The Saga of the Volsungs* (Berkeley, CA: University of California Press, 1990).

Cavill, Paul, 'Interpretation of *The Battle of Maldon*, Lines 84–90: A Review and Reassessment', *Studia Neophilologica*, 67 (1995), 149–64.

Chen, Fanfan and Thomas Honegger (eds), *Good Dragons are Rare. An Inquiry into Literary Dragons East and West*, ALPH 5 (Frankfurt am Main: Peter Lang, 2009).

Curley, Michael J. (ed. and trans.), *Physiologus. A Medieval Book of Nature Lore* (Chicago: The University of Chicago Press, 1979, repr. 2009).

Cutrer, Robert E., 'The Wilderness of Dragons. The Reception of Dragons in Thirteenth-century Iceland' (unpublished MA thesis, University of Iceland, 2012).

de Visser, Marinus Willem, *The Dragon in China and Japan* (Amsterdam: J. Müller, 1913).

Devlin, James Dacres, *The Mordiford Dragon, to which is added The Priest, Lady, and Bailiff; a tale of Hereford of the time of the Conquest: as also, The Verses on the Aged 'Aunt Bess'* (Hereford: Printed by C. Anthony, Widemarsh-Street, 1848).

Dickinson, Peter, *The Flight of Dragons* (New York: Harper & Row, 1979).

Evans, Jonathan D., 'Semiotics and Traditional Lore: The Medieval Dragon Tradition', *Journal of Folklore Research*, 22 (1985), 85–112.

——, 'The Dragon', in Malcolm South (ed.), *Mythical and Fabulous Creatures: A Source Book and Research Guide* (New York: Bedrick, 1988), pp. 27–58.

——, '"As Rare As They Are Dire?" Old Norse Dragons, *Beowulf*, and the *Deutsche Mythologie*', in Tom Shippey (ed.), *The Shadow-Walkers: Jacob Grimm's Mythology of the Monstrous*, Medieval and Renaissance Texts and Studies 291 (Tempe, AZ: Arizona Center for Medieval and Renaissance Studies/Turnhout: Brepols, 2005), pp. 207–69.

Fairbairn, James, *Fairbairn's Book of Crests of the Families of Great Britain and Ireland*, 2 vols (1859; 4th, rev. and expanded edn; London: TC & EC Jack, 1905).

Feierabend, M. A., 'Der Luzerner Drachenstein', *Verhandlungen der Schweizerischen Naturforschenden Gesellschaft*, 46 (1862), 89–97.

Fellows, Jennifer, '"Dragons two other thre": The Dragon Motif in Some Middle English Romances' (unpublished manuscript).

—— (ed.), *Bevis of Hampton*, 2 vols, Early English Text Society Original Series 349 and 350 (Oxford: Oxford University Press, 2017).

Fonterose, Joseph, *Python: A Study of Delphic Myth and its Origins* (Berkeley: University of California Press, 1959).

Forest-Hill, Lynn (trans.), *Bevis of Hampton* (Southampton: So: To Speak/Southampton Festivals, in association with Gumbo Press, 2015).

——, 'Fantasy Elements in Medieval Romance: History or Imagination?', *Yearbook of Eastern European Studies*, 6 (2016), 61–76.

Fulk, Robert D., Robert E. Bjork and John D. Niles (eds), *Klaeber's Beowulf* (4th edn; Toronto: University of Toronto Press, 2008).

Gneuss, Helmut, '*The Battle of Maldon* 89: Byrhtnoð's *ofermod* Once Again', in Katherine O'Brien O'Keeffe (ed.), *Old English Shorter Poems: Basic Readings* (New York and London: Garland Publishing, 1994), pp. 149–72.

Goth, Maik, 'Spenser's Dragons', in Fanfan Chen and Thomas Honegger (eds), *Good Dragons are Rare. An Inquiry into Literary Dragons East and West*, ALPH 5 (Frankfurt am Main: Peter Lang, 2009), pp. 97–117.

Gourarier, Zeev, Philippe Hoch and Patrick Absalon (eds), *Dragons. Au jardin zoologique des mythologies* (Metz: Éditions Serpenoise, 2005).

Grahame, Kenneth, *The Reluctant Dragon* (repr. of the 1938 edn; originally pub. 1898; New York: Holiday House, 1989).

Hammer, Andreas, 'Der heilige Drachentöter: Transformationen eines Strukturmusters', in Andreas Hammer and Stephanie Seidel (eds), *Helden und Heilige. Kulturelle und literarische Integrationsfiguren des europäischen Mittelalters* (Heidelberg: Universitätsverlag Winter, 2010), pp. 143–79.

Hanlon, Tina L., 'The Taming of the Dragon in Twentieth-Century Picture Books', *Journal of the Fantastic in the Arts*, 14/1 (2003), 7–26.

Herzman, Ronald B., Graham Drake and Eve Salisbury (eds), *Four Romances of England. King Horn, Havelok the Dane, Bevis of Hampton, Athelston*, TEAMS Middle English Series (Kalamazoo, MI: Medieval Institute Publications, 1999).

Honegger, Thomas, 'The Man in the Moon: Structural Depth in Tolkien', in Thomas Honegger (ed.), *Root & Branch: Approaches towards Understanding Tolkien* (1999; Zurich and Berne: Walking Tree Publishers, 2005), pp. 9–70.

——, '*Draco litterarius*: Some Thoughts on an Imaginary Beast', in Sabine Obermaier (ed.), *Tiere und Fabelwesen im Mittelalter* (Berlin and New York: Walter de Gruyter, 2009), pp. 133–45.

——, 'From Bestiary onto Screen: Dragons in Film', in Renate Bauer and Ulrike Krischke (eds), *Fact and Fiction: From the Middle Ages to Modern Times. Essays Presented to Hans Sauer on*

the Occasion of his 65th Birthday, Texte und Untersuchungen zur Englischen Philologie 37 (Frankfurt am Main: Peter Lang, 2011), pp. 197–215.

—, 'Der Drache: Herausforderer von Heiligen und Helden', in Luca Tori and Aline Steinbrecher (eds), *Animali: Tiere und Fabelwesen von der Antike bis zur Neuzeit* (Geneva and Milano: Skira, 2012), pp. 192–203.

—, 'Allegorical Hares and Real Dragons – Animals in Medieval Literature and Beyond', in Roman Bartosch (ed.), *Animal Poetics* (special issue of *Anglistik*, 27/2 (2016), 47–57).

—, 'Transformations of Fairy Stories: From *Sellic/Sælig Spell* to *Beowulf*, or from Folk Tale to Epic', *Hither Shore*, 12 (2016), 248–60.

—, 'The Sea-dragon – in Search of an Elusive Creature', in Gerlinde Huber-Rebenich, Christian Rohr and Michael Stolz (eds), *Wasser in der mittelalterlichen Kultur / Water in Medieval Culture* (Berlin: de Gruyter, 2017), pp. 221–31.

—, 'Zoology', in *Routledge Medieval Encyclopedia Online* (forthcoming, 2019).

Hudson, Harriet (ed.), *Four Middle English Romances: Sir Isumbras, Octavian, Sir Eglamour of Artois, Sir Tryamour*, TEAMS Middle English Series (Kalamazoo, MI: Medieval Institute Publications, 2006).

Hume, Kathryn, 'From Saga to Romance: The Use of Monsters in Old Norse Literature', *Studies in Philology*, 77 (1980), 1–25.

Ireland, Samuel, *Picturesque Views on the River Wye* (London: Published by R. Faulder, New Bond Street; and T. Egerton, Whitehall, 1797).

Isidore of Seville, *The Etymologies of Isidore of Seville*, ed. and trans. Stephen A. Barney, W. J. Lewis, J. A. Beach and Oliver Berhof, in collaboration with Muriel Hall (Cambridge: Cambridge University Press, 2006).

Jacobs, Nicolas, 'Sir *Degarré*, *Lay le Freine*, *Beves of Hamtoun*, and the "Auchinleck Bookshop"', *Notes and Queries*, 227 (1982), 294–301.

Jacobus de Voragine, *Legenda Aurea* (*c.*1275; translated into English by William Caxton 1483. Available at *https://sourcebooks.fordham.edu/basis/goldenlegend/* (accessed 24 July 2018)).

Jakobsson, Ármann, 'Enter the Dragon: Legendary Saga Courage and the Birth of the Hero', in Martin Arnold and Alison Finlay (eds), *Making History: Essays on the fornaldarsögur*, Viking Society for Northern Research (Exeter: Short Run Press Limited, 2010), pp. 33–52.

Joger, Ulrich and Jochen Luckhardt (eds), *Schlangen und Drachen. Kunst und Natur* (Darmstadt: WGB, 2007).

Jones, David, *An Instinct for Dragons* (New York: Routledge, 2000).

King, Andrew, *The Faerie Queene and Middle English Romance: The Matter of Just Memory* (Oxford: Clarendon Press, 2000).

Klegraf, J., W. Kühlwein, D. Nehls and R. Zimmermann (eds), *Beowulf und die kleineren Denkmäler der altenglischen Heldensage Waldere und Finnsburg. 1. Teil: Text, Übersetzung und Stammtafeln* (Heidelberg: Carl Winter, 1976).

Koch, Sebastian, *Der Kampf des Helden gegen den egeslîchen trachen. Zur narrativen Funktion des Topos vom Drachenkampf in vergleichender Perspektive* (Göppingen: Kümmerle Verlag, 2016).

Kordecki, Lesley Catherine, 'Traditions and Development of the Medieval English Dragon' (unpublished PhD thesis, University of Toronto, Centre for Medieval Studies, 1980).

——, 'Losing the Monster and Recovering the Non-human in Fable(d) Subjectivity', in L. A. H. R. Houwen (ed.), *Animals and the Symbolic in Mediaeval Art and Literature* (Groningen: Egbert Forsten, 1997), pp. 25–37.

Kuehn, Sara, *The Dragon in Medieval East Christian and Islamic Art*, Islamic History and Civilization 86 (Leiden and Boston: Brill, 2011).

Lang, Andrew (ed.), *The Red Fairy Book* (4th edn; London: Longmans, Green & Co., 1893).

Laskaya, Anne and Eve Salisbury (eds), *The Middle English Breton Lays*, TEAMS Middle English Text Series (Kalamazoo, MI: Medieval Institute Publications, 1995).

Le Goff, Jacques, 'Ecclesiastical Culture and Folklore in the Middle Ages: Saint Marcellus of Paris and the Dragon', in Jacques Le Goff, *Time, Work, and Culture in the Middle Ages*, trans. Arthur Goldhammer (Chicago and London: The University of Chicago Press, 1980), pp. 159–88.

Leclercq-Marx, Jacqueline, 'Le dragon comme métaphore des démons intérieurs. Mots et images', in Danielle Buschinger and Wolfgang Spiewok (eds), *Le dragon dans la culture médiévale*, Wodan 39 (Greifswald: Reineke-Verlag, 1994), pp. 45–56.

Lecouteux, Claude, 'Der Drache', *Zeitschrift für deutsches Altertum und deutsche Literatur*, 108 (1979), 13–31.

Lionarons, Joyce Tally, *The Medieval Dragon. The Nature of the Beast in Germanic Literature* (Enfield Lock: Hisarlik Press, 1998).

——, '"Sometimes the Dragon Wins": Unsuccessful Dragon Fighters in Medieval Literature', in Loren C. Gruber, Meredith Crellin Gruber and Gregory K. Jember (eds), *Essays on Old, Middle, Modern English and Old Icelandic* (Lewiston, NY: The Edwin Mellen Press, 2000), pp. 301–16.

Lipscombe, George, *Journey into South Wales, through the counties of Oxford, Warwick, Worcester, Hereford, Salop, Stafford, Buckingham, and Hertford; in the year* 1799 (London: Printed by A. Strahan, Printers Street, for T. N. Longman & O. Rees, Paternoster Row, 1802).

Lupack, Alan (ed.), *Lancelot of the Laik and Sir Tristrem*, TEAMS Middle English Series (Kalamazoo, MI: Medieval Institute Publications, 1994).

McConnell, Winder, 'Mythos Drache', in Ulrich Müller and Werner Wunderlich (eds), *Dämonen, Monster, Fabelwesen*, Mittelalter Mythen 2 (St. Gallen: UVK, 1999), pp. 171–83.

Michel, Paul, *Tiere als Symbol und Ornament* (Wiesbaden: Ludwig Reichert Verlag, 1979).

——, 'Was zur Beglaubigung dieser Historie dienen mag: Drachen bei Johann Jacob Scheuchzer', in Fanfan Chen and Thomas Honegger (eds), *Good Dragons are Rare. An Inquiry into Literary Dragons East and West*, ALPH 5 (Frankfurt am Main: Peter Lang, 2009), 119–70.

Milton, John, *Paradise Lost* (1667). Available at *https://www.dartmouth.edu/~milton/reading_room/pl/book_1/text.shtml* (accessed 10 October 2018).

Neckam, Alexander, *De naturis rerum libri duo*, ed. Thomas Wright, Rolls Series 34 (London: Longman, Green, Longman, Roberts and Green, 1863).

Ogden, Daniel, *Dragons, Serpents, and Slayers in the Classical and Early Christian Worlds. A Sourcebook* (Oxford and New York: Oxford University Press, 2013).

Okken, Lambertus, 'Zur Stammesgeschichte des europäischen Märchendrachen', *Fabula*, 26 (1985), 80–97.

Page, Sophie, 'Good Creation and Demonic Illusions: The Medieval Universe of Creatures', in Linda Kalof and Brigitte Resl (eds), *A Cultural History of Animals. Volume 2: The Medieval Age* (1000–1400) (London: Bloomsbury, 2007), pp. 27–57.

Petty, Anne C., *Dragons of Fantasy* (2nd edn; Crawfordville FL: Kitsune Books, 2008).

Price, Jocelyn, 'The Virgin and the Dragon: The Demonology of *Seinte Margarete*', *Leeds Studies in English*, NS 16 (1985), 337–57.

Privat, Jean-Marie (ed.), *Dragons – entre science et fictions* (Paris: CNRS, 2006).

Rauer, Christine, *Beowulf and the Dragon. Parallels and Analogues* (Woodbridge: D. S. Brewer, 2000).

Reinle, Adolf, *Die Kunstdenkmäler des Kantons Luzern. Band II. Die Stadt Luzern: I. Teil* (Basel: Birkhäuser, 1953).

—, 'Volkskundliches in den Luzerner Kunstdenkmälern', *Schweizerisches Archiv für Volkskunde*, 51 (1955), 93–102.

Riches, Samantha J., *St George. Hero, Martyr and Myth* (Stroud: Sutton Publishing, 2000).

—, 'Encountering the Monstrous: Saints and Dragons in Medieval Thought', in Bettina Bildhauer and Robert Mills (eds), *The Monstrous Middle Ages* (Cardiff: University of Wales Press, 2003), pp. 196–218.

Roling, Bernd, *Drachen und Sirenen. Die Rationalisierung und Abwicklung der Mythologie an den europäischen Universitäten* (Leiden and Boston: Brill, 2010).

Sagan, Carl, *The Dragons of Eden* (New York: Random House, 1977).

Schneidewind, Friedhelm, *Drachen. Das Schmöcker-Lexikon* (Saarbrücken: Verlag der Villa Fledermaus, 2008).

Seel, Otto (ed. and trans.), *Der Physiologus* (Zurich: Artemis, 1992).

Senter, Phil, Uta Mattox and Eid E. Haddad, 'Snake to Monster: Conrad Gessner's *Schlangenbuch* and the Evolution of the Dragon in the Literature of Natural History', *Journal of Folklore Research*, 53/1 (2016), 67–124.

Shippey, Tom A., *Poems of Wisdom and Learning in Old English* (Cambridge: D.S. Brewer, 1976).

—, *Laughing Shall I Die. Lives and Deaths of the Great Vikings* (London: Reaktion Books, 2018).

Shuker, Karl, *Dragons: A Natural History* (New York: McGraw-Hill, 1995).

Simpson, Jacqueline, 'Fifty British Dragon Tales: An Analysis', *Folklore*, 89 (1978), 79–93.

—, *British Dragons* (1980; Ware: Wordsworth, 2001).

Slade, Benjamin (ed. and trans.), *Beowulf: Diacritically Marked Text and Facing Translation*, *http://www.heorot.dk/beo-intro-rede.html*, 2002–12 (accessed 25 August 2018).

Spearing, A. C., *Medieval Dream-Poetry* (Cambridge: Cambridge University Press, 1976).

Steer, Dugald A. (ed.), *Dr. Ernest Drake's Dragonology. The Complete Book of Dragons* (Somerville, MA: Candlewick Press, 2003).

Tolkien, J. R. R., 'The Dragon's Visit', *Oxford Magazine* 55/1 (4 February 1937), 342.

— and Eric Valentine Gordon (eds), *Sir Gawain and the Green Knight*, 2nd edn ed. Norman Davies (1925; Oxford: Clarendon Press, 1967).

— (trans.), *Sir Gawain and the Green Knight, Pearl, and Sir Orfeo*, ed. Christopher Tolkien (1975; London: HarperCollins, 1995).

—, 'Beowulf: The Monsters and the Critics', in J. R. R. Tolkien, *The Monsters and the Critics and Other Essays*, ed. Christopher Tolkien (London: HarperCollins, 1997), pp. 5–48.

—, *The Letters of* J. R. R. *Tolkien*, ed. Humphrey Carpenter, with the assistance of Christopher Tolkien (1981; Boston: Houghton Mifflin, 2000).

—, *The Children of Húrin*, ed. Christopher Tolkien (London: HarperCollins, 2007).

—, *Tolkien On Fairy-stories*, ed. Verlyn Flieger and Douglas A. Anderson (London: HarperCollins, 2008).

—, *Beowulf. A Translation and Commentary together with Sellic Spell*, ed. Christopher Tolkien (London: HarperCollins, 2014).

Topsell, Edward, *The History of Four-footed Beasts and Serpents* (London: Printed by E. Cotes, 1658).

Trevisa, John, *On the Properties of Things. John Trevisa's translation of Bartholomaeus Anglicus De Proprietatibus Rerum*, ed. M. Seymour et al., 3 vols (Oxford: Clarendon Press, vols I and II Text: 1975, vol. III Commentary: 1988).

Völsunga Saga, ed. Guðni Jónsson and Bjarni Vilhjálmsson, *http://heimskringla.no/wiki/Völsunga_saga* (accessed 24 July 2018).

Watkins, Calvert, *How to Kill a Dragon. Aspects of Indo-European Poetics* (Oxford: Oxford University Press, 1995).

Weiss, Judith, 'The Major Interpolations in *Sir Beues of Hamtoun*', *Medium Ævum*, 48 (1979), 71–6.

White, Terence Hanbury (ed. and trans.), *The Book of Beasts. Being a Translation from a Latin Bestiary of the Twelfth Century* (1st edn 1954; Stroud: Alan Sutton, 1992).

Zhao, Qiguang, *A Study of Dragons, East and West*, Asian Thought and Culture 11 (New York: Peter Lang, 1992).

INDEX

A

Aldrovandi, Ulisse (AD 1522–1605; author of *Historia animalium*) 20
allegory; allegorical interpretation 22–5, 40, 48, 88, 101, 109, 117
Augustine of Hippo (AD 354–430) 24–5

B

Bartholomaeus Anglicus (AD *c.*1190–*c.*1270; author of *De proprietas rerum*) 20–1
  see also Trevisa
Beowulf (Old English epic poem) 3–4, 6, 7, 78, 83–93
Beowulf-dragon 3–5, 31, 84–93
Bevis of Hampton (Middle English romance) 98–113

C

Cauldron of Story 67–9, 78

D

Daniel (biblical prophet) 39, 76
Sir Degaré (Middle English romance) 95–6
dragon
  Chinese dragons 56, 58–61, 118
  detailed description 102–5
  as devil/Satan 37, 39, 40, 52, 55, 108
  and elephant 27–9, 32
  in encyclopaedias 20–1, 25–7, 29–31
  as *maximum obstaculum* (greatest challenge) 93–5, 99
  Mordiford dragon 68–79
  in mythology 12–13
  and natural science 17–21
  in paganism 42, 46–7
  and parody 95–7, 118
  poison 27, 29–32, 42, 46, 72–3, 92, 107–8
  prototypical characteristics and features 4–5
  and saints 41–52
  single combat 102
  as snake in Paradise 55–6

dragon (*cont.*)
tail 105–7
terminology and etymology 6–8
theories explaining origin 10–11
tongue 72, 105, 112
types 7–10

E

Eglamour of Artois (Middle English romance) 93–4
Erec and Enide (Old French romanc) 95

F

Fafnir 6, 31, 67, 76, 85

G

Gessner, Conrad (AD 1516–65; author of *Historia animalum*) 20
Grahame, Kenneth (AD 1859–1932; author of 'The Reluctant Dragon') 47, 118

H

hoard 4–5, 84–5

I

Isidore of Seville (AD 560–636; author of *Etymologiae*) 26–7, 29–30

K

killing a dragon
detailed description of fight 110–12
in a non-chivalric manner 95–7
in single combat 88–93
as stock narrative element 93–5, 97
with a trick 74–6

L

Leviathan 12, 39
Linnaeus, Carolus (AD 1707–78; author of *Regnum animale*) 17–21

M

Mary (as woman of the Apocalypse) 54–6
Maxims II (Old English poem) 5
Midgard Serpent 12
Mordiford (and the Mordiford dragon/wyfern) 68–79

P

Pelican 23–5
Physiologus 22–3
Pliny the Elder (AD 23–79) 29
Python 13

R

Ragnar Lothbrok 76
Reign of Fire (2002) 117

S

Saints (and dragons) 41–2
Saint George 42–9, 61
Saint Marcellus of Paris 46
Saint Margaret of Antioch 45, 48, 50–2
Saint Martha 45
Saint Michael 41

Saint Samson of Dol 46
Saint Sylvester of Rome 46, 52
Sigurd/Siegfried 6, 67
Sir Gawain and the Green Knight (Middle English romance) 97
Smaug 86
Spenser, Edmund (AD 1552–99; author of *The Faerie Queene*) 98, 113
Switzerland 56, 59–60, 72

T

tail (of the dragon) 105–7
Thomas of Cantimpré (AD 1201–72; author of *Liber de natura rerum*) 21
Tiamat 12
Tolkien, John Ronald Reuel (AD 1892–1973) 47, 79, 118
tongue (of the dragon) 72, 105, 112
Topsell, Edward (AD 1572–1625; author of *The History of the Four-footed Beasts and Serpents*) 20
Trevisa, John (AD 1342–1402; author of *On the Properties of Things*) 30–3
Tristan 31
Typhon 13

V

Vincent of Beauvais (AD 1184–1264; author of *Speculum naturale*) 21